Readings in Literary Criticism   13

CRITICS ON GEORGE ELIOT

Readings in Literary Criticism

1. CRITICS ON KEATS
2. CRITICS ON CHARLOTTE AND EMILY BRONTE
3. CRITICS ON POPE
4. CRITICS ON MARLOWE
5. CRITICS ON JANE AUSTEN   Edited by Judish O'Neill
6. CRITICS ON CHAUCER   Edited by Sheila Sullivan
7. CRITICS ON BLAKE   Edited by Judith O'Neill
8. CRITICS ON VIRGINIA WOOLF   Edited by Jacqueline Latham
9. CRITICS ON D. H. LAWRENCE   Edited by W. T. Andrews
10. CRITICS ON YEATS   Edited by Raymond Cowell
11. CRITICS ON MATTHEW ARNOLD   Edited by Jacqueline Latham
12. CRITICS ON WORDSWORTH   Edited by Raymond Cowell
13. CRITICS ON GEORGE ELIOT   Edited by William Baker
14. CRITICS ON T. S. ELIOT   Edited by Sheila Sullivan
15. CRITICS ON DRYDEN   Edited by Robert McHenry and David G. Lougee
16. CRITICS ON SHAKESPEARE   Edited by W. T. Andrews

CRITICS ON GEORGE ELIOT

Readings in Literary Criticism

Edited by William Baker

London · George Allen & Unwin Ltd

PRINTED IN GREAT BRITAIN
in 10 *on* 11 *pt Plantin type*
BY CLARKE, DOBLE & BRENDON LIMITED
PLYMOUTH

CONTENTS

INTRODUCTION   *page* vii

ACKNOWLEDGEMENTS   ix

CRITICS ON GEORGE ELIOT: 1856–1953

George Eliot, Elizabeth Gaskell, Leo Tolstoy, W. Lucas
Collins, Sir Edward Bulwer-Lytton, John Ruskin, Henry
James, Robert Browning, F. T. Palgrave, A. G. Sedgewick,
John Blackwood, Richard Holt Hutton, Samuel Butler,
Emily Dickinson, Lord Acton, Joseph Jacobs, Anthony
Trollope, George Henry Lewes, Robert L. Stevenson,
Sigmund Freud, Leslie Stephen, Henry James, Virginia
Woolf, J. W. Beach, T. S. Eliot and three anonymous
contemporary reviewers.

MODERN CRITICS ON GEORGE ELIOT   59

JEROME BEATY   *Middlemarch*: The Writing of Chapter 81   59

DAVID DAICHES   George Eliot   72

ROBERT PREYER   Beyond the Liberal Imagination: Vision
                           and Unreality in *Daniel Deronda*   77

FRED C. THOMSON   *Felix Holt* as Classic Tragedy   84

IAN GREGOR   The Two Worlds of *Adam Bede*   91

CAROLE ROBINSON   *Romola*: A Reading of the Novel   96

DAVID R. CARROLL   *Silas Marner*: Reversing the Oracles of
                           Religion   104

U. C. KNOEPFLMACHER   *Scenes of Clerical Life*   109

SELECT BIBLIOGRAPHY   112

INTRODUCTION

Criticism of George Eliot's works divides into three periods: that of her contemporaries; a lengthy period, in which her star was on the wane, lasting from her death in 1881 until about 1940; and the most recent. Contemporaries saw George Eliot as a sage and moralist despite her liaison with George Henry Lewes. Their reverence for the serious, guru, side of her art had much to do with their own search for faith. The frequently cited George Eliot observation that 'Duty' was 'peremptory and absolute', that 'God' was 'inconceivable', 'Immortality' was 'unbelievable' is indicative of many Victorian obsessions. These are also reflected by Richard Holt Hutton's emphasis (in his great review of *Middlemarch*) on George Eliot's seriousness and her melancholy.

Victorian criticism may appear difficult to read, yet some of the earliest reactions to George Eliot are among the most valuable. The language of criticism may have changed but the essential points have not. The main difference is that Victorians were apt to tell the story, whereas modern critics expect the work to have been read and concentrate on specialized aspects of it. An additional interest is that critics such as the anonymous reviewer of *Adam Bede*, and the Rev. Lucas Collins writing on *The Mill*, consciously allow social and moral attitudes to colour their views, so that reading them tells us much about George Eliot's society and her critics' attitudes.

The formulation of Victorian critical responses can be seen in the reactions to each work as it appeared. The relatively straightforward praise of *The Saturday Review* for 'the truthfulness of the characters and incidents' in *Scenes of Clerical Life*, also mentions 'pathos'. The reviewer's admiration for the realism of *Adam Bede* turns into moral questioning. In *Silas Marner* 'it is impossible to say which is the most admirable, the vivid painting of life itself, or the profound remarks on the progress of that life!' A. G. Sedgewick, in his response to *Felix Holt*' and those greatest of the Victorian critics of George Eliot, Henry James and Richard Hutton, find fault with her technique. The critic of *Daniel Deronda* is already engaged in a long rearguard action against its detractors. Critical debate changes little: *Romola* is still taken to be a failure and still finds its defenders; *Felix Holt* still occupies an ambivalent position critically; the Jewish parts of *Daniel Deronda* are either ignored or treated as inferior to the rest of the book. Occasional private remarks are often as illuminating as pages of sophisticated criticism. Samuel Butler confessed to finding *Middlemarch* 'long-winded'. Stevenson looked upon George Eliot as 'a rather dry lady'. In our century T. S. Eliot was scared by Rosamund Vincy. In 1881 Ruskin commented that *The Mill* reminded him of 'the sweepings out of a Pentonville omnibus'.

Even in the long lean years which followed her death George Eliot had her supporters, who debated the perennial problem of which of her novels deserved the highest accolade. Leslie Stephen found *Middlemarch* 'painful' (and the now unjustly neglected *Spanish Gypsy* and miscellaneous poetry of interest), yet his daughter, Virginia Woolf, found George Eliot's power at its highest in that novel. They both appreciated contemporary arguments that George Eliot was too long-winded, too moralistic, and yet, together with Henry James, recognized the debt which the Novel owed to her. The impact of Freud and Joyce in America led such critics as Beach in the thirties and Schorer in the forties to point to her psychological penetration and use of imagery. But it was not until the work of S. L. Bethell, Joan Bennett, and F. R. Leavis, among others, appeared in the late thirties and forties that George Eliot began to achieve the prominence she now has.

Modern criticism can be divided into two periods: before and after the appearance of G. S. Haight's edition of *The George Eliot Letters* in 1954–6. The letters threw light upon George Eliot's life, thoughts, fiction source materials and so much more, and they provide the basis for subsequent criticism. The criticism of the late fifties and early sixties represented by such well-known and perceptive works as Barbara Hardy's *The Novels of George Eliot: A Study in Form*, 1959, and W. J. Harvey's *The Art of George Eliot*, 1961, concentrated on the formalistic aspects of her work and their influence is to be seen in the essays of I. Gregor and D. Carroll. Carole Robinson's response to *Romola*, R. Preyer's indication of areas of interest in neglected parts of *Daniel Deronda*, and U. C. Knoepflmacher's philosophical orientation towards the earliest works, each illustrate aspects opened up by the *Letters*. D. Daiches' general observations are representative of modern opinion as a whole. Although F. Thomson's article appeared as long ago as 1961, it reflects an area of work on George Eliot which, with notable exceptions (especially that of Jerome Beaty on *Middlemarch*), is only now beginning to attract attention: that is the study of her texts, manuscript revisions and notebooks.

One of the fascinations of criticism is that fashionable views are challenged, undercurrents of opinion become mainstreams and then they in turn are challenged. It is worth remembering when reading George Eliot that one of her firm beliefs was that we see only what we wish to see, and that much is relative in criticism as in life.

Department of English
The University of the Negev

William Baker

ACKNOWLEDGEMENTS

We are grateful to the following for permission to use copyright material from the works whose titles follow in brackets:

The Hograth Press Ltd (Ernest Jones's *The Life and Work of Sigmund Freud*); The Hogarth Press Ltd ('George Eliot' from *The Common Reader* by Virginia Woolf); Appleton-Century-Crofts (J. W. Beach's *The Twentieth Century Novel: Studies in Technique*); Faber and Faber Ltd (T. S. Eliot's 'Three Voices of Poetry' from *On Poetry and Poets*); University of Illinois Press (Jerome Beaty's *Middlemarch from Notebook to Novel*); Secker and Warburg Ltd (David Daiches's *A Critical History of English Literature*, Second Edition, Vol. 2); University of Indiana (Robert Preyer's 'Beyond the Liberal Imagination: Vision and Unreality in *Daniel Deronda*' from *Victorian Studies*, Vol. 4, 1960); University of California Press (Fred C. Thomson's '*Felix Holt* as Classic Tragedy'. Copyright © 1961 by The Regents of the University of California. Reprinted from *Nineteenth-Century Fiction*, Vol. 16, No. 1, by permission of The Regents); Faber and Faber Ltd (Ian Gregor and Brian Nicholas: 'The Two Worlds of *Adam Bede*' from *The Moral And The Story*); University of Indiana (Carole Robinson's '*Romola*: A Reading of the Novel' from *Victorian Studies*, Vol 6, 1962); The University of Wisconsin Press (David R. Carroll's '*Silas Marner*: Reversing the Oracles of Religion', *Literary Monographs*, Vol. 1, 1967. Copyright © 1967 by the Regents of the University of Wisconsin); University of California Press (U. C. Kneopflmacher's *George Eliot's Early Novels: The Limits of Realism*, 1968. Originally published by the University of California Press; reprinted by permission of The Regents of the University of California).

Critics on George Eliot
1856-1953

GEORGE ELIOT: 1856; 1860; 1861; 1863; 1871; 1876
Some Comments from Her Reviews and Letters

... The greatest benefit we owe to the artist ... is the extension of
our sympathies ... Art is the nearest thing to life; it is a mode of
amplifying experience and extending our contact with our fellow-men
beyond the bounds of our personal lot. All the more sacred is the task of
the artists when he undertakes to paint the life of the People. ...

> From a review, 'The Natural History of German Life', *The West-
> minster Review*, Vol. 66, July 1856, pp. 51–79 (54).

> (The page numbers before the bracket give the beginning and end
> of the whole article; those within the bracket the pages of the actual
> extract.)

... On two points I recognize the justice of his criticism. [Sir Edward
Bulwer-Lytton on *The Mill on the Floss*]. First, that Maggie is made to
appear too passive in the scene of quarrel in the Red Deeps ...
Secondly, that the tragedy is not adequately prepared. ... The other
chief point of criticism—Maggie's position towards Stephen—is too
vital a part of my whole conception and purpose for me to be converted
to the condemnation of it. ... If the ethics of art do not admit the
truthful presentation of a character essentially noble but liable to great
error—error that is anguish to its own nobleness—*then* ... the ethics of
art ... must be widened to correspond with a widening psychology. ...

> From a letter to her publisher, John Blackwood, 9 July 1860, in
> G. S. Haight, *The George Eliot Letters*, Vol. 3, Oxford and Yale,
> 1954–6, pp. 317–18. For Bulwer-Lytton's criticism see p. 15.

... I have faith in the working-out of higher possibilities than the
Catholic or any other church has presented, and those who have the
strength to wait and endure, are bound to accept no formula which
their whole souls—their intellect as well as their emotions—do not
embrace with entire reverence. The highest 'calling and election' is to

do without opium and live through all our pain with conscious, clear-eyed endurance . . .

From a letter to her friend, Mme Eugene Bodichon, Boxing Day 1860, *Ibid.*, Vol. 3, p. 366.

. . . I don't wonder at your finding [*Silas Marner*] rather sombre . . . But I hope that you will not find it all a sad story, as a whole, since it sets—or is intended to set—in a strong light the remedial influences of pure, natural human relations. The Nemesis is a mild one . . .

From a letter to Blackwood, 24 February 1861, *Ibid.*, Vol. 3, p. 382.

. . . It is the habit of my imagination to strive after as full a vision of the medium in which a character moves as of the character itself. The psychological causes which prompted me to give such details of Florentine life and history as I have given, are precisely the same as those which determined me in giving the details of English village life in *Silas Marner*, or the 'Dodson' life, out of which were developed the destinies of poor Tom and Maggie. But you have correctly pointed out the reason why my tendency to excess in this effort after artistic vision makes the impression of a fault in *Romola* much more perceptibly than in my previous books. And I am not surprised at your dissatisfaction with Romola herself. I can well believe that the many difficulties, belonging to the treatment of such a character have not been overcome, and that I have failed to bring out my conception with adequate fullness. I am sorry she has attracted you so little. . . .

From a letter to the critic Richard Holt Hutton, 8 August 1863, *Ibid.*, Vol. 4, p. 97.

. . . I don't see how I can leave anything out of [*Middlemarch*] because I hope there is nothing that will be seen to be irrelevant to my design, which is to show the gradual action of ordinary causes rather than exceptional, and to show this in some directions which have not been from time immemorial the beaten path—the Cremorne walks and shows of fiction . . .

From a letter to Blackwood, 24 July 1871, *Ibid.*, Vol. 5, p. 168.

. . . my writing is simply a set of experiments in life—an endeavour to see what our thought and emotion may be capable of—what stores of motive, actual or hinted as possible, give promise of a better after which we may strive—what gains from past revelations and discipline we must strive to keep hold of as something more than shifting theory. I become more and more timid—with less daring to adopt any formula which does not get itself clothed for me in some human figure and individual experience, and perhaps that is a sign that if I help others to see at all it must be through that medium of art.

From a letter to the physician Dr J. F. Payne, 25 January 1876, *Ibid.*, Vol. 6, p. 216.

... readers ... cut the book [*Daniel Deronda*] into scraps and talk of nothing in it but Gwendolen. I meant everything in the book to be related to everything else there. ...

From a letter to Mme Bodichon, 2 October 1876, *Ibid.*, Vol. 6, p. 290.

ANONYMOUS: 1858
'Scenes of Clerical Life' A New Novelist

George Eliot is a new novelist, who to rare culture adds rare faculty, who can paint homely every-day life and ordinary characters with great humour and pathos, and is content to rely on the truth of his pictures for effect ... 'The Sad Fortunes of the Rev. Amos Barton' gives us the picture of a curate who, on eighty pounds a year, has to support a wife and six children in decency, and to minister to the spiritual wants of a congregation. Here is a subject thoroughly common-place. The man himself is wholly commonplace. Yet the story is not only interesting, but perfectly fresh and original—the character is not only a distinct individuality, but one which appeals to and wins our deepest sympathy. We do not admire Barton; indeed we rather laugh at him; yet the laughter is tempered by sympathy and we like him for the same reasons that we like many other commonplace people—because of his charming wife, his charming children, his misfortunes, and his position. He is not handsome, he is not wise, he is not even nobly virtuous. . . . To make a hero out of such a curate required steadfast faith in the power of truth, and disregard of conventions. The same disregard of circu-lating-library principles is seen in the portrait of the Rev. Mr. Gilfil, whose love story forms the second of these sketches. We are introduced to Mr. Gilfil when he is old ... but instead of our being called upon to weep over a wasted life, and to pity a noble ruin, we are forced to love and admire a quite ordinary mortal, caustic, benevolent, active, some-what miserly, and given to the evening solace of a pipe and gin-and-water. . . .

Once more is the boldness of this writer shown in his choice of 'Janet's Repentance'—the third and finest of these *Clerical Scenes*. He calls upon us to accept as a heroine a woman driven by ill-treatment and misery to that unpoetical, but unhappily too real, refuge—wine! This tragic sin is dealt with at once delicately and boldly; and the story of her repentance and victory is one of the most pathetic scenes we know. A beautiful, impulsive, loving woman is shown us in her sin and in her rescue; and the influence exerted over her mind by the sympathetic earnestness of the Rev. Mr. Tryan—whose persecutions and sorrows also form an important element in the story—is represented in a style so truthful that we seem to be reading an actual biography.

While commending the truthfulness of the characters and incidents, we must make one exception. The episode of Mr. Tryan's early love and sorrow is a great mistake. It is one of the incidents hackneyed in fiction; and we are surprised to find it among incidents so fresh as those of the *Clerical Scenes*. Another objection we must urge, although it is purely technical. In 'Mr. Gilfil's Love Story' a great mistake in art is made in the construction—there are no less than three retrospects in it. One if enough, in all conscience. When the story fairly commences, it proceeds with due rapidity.

As might have been expected, a writer who selects topics so unlike those of other novelists, and who disregards conventions in conception, will not be likely to fall into the slipslop and conventions of expression which make the generality of novels difficult to read twice. In no page of these volumes have we noticed writing for writing's sake, or phrases flung out at hazard. The language always expresses distinct ideas, and the epithets are chosen because they are fitting. Indeed, so far from carelessness being the fault of the style, we should rather urge the objection of a too constant elaboration, especially in the earlier pages, where almost every sentence seems finished into an epigram or an aphorism. The pudding is often too profuse in plums—too scanty in connective dough. Instead of simply referring to the village organist, he refers to 'a collector of small rents, differentiated by the force of circumstances into an organist;' the curate's hat 'shows no symptoms of taking to the hideous doctrine of expediency, and shaping itself according to circumstances;' and 'the human animal of the male sex was understood to be perpetually athirst, and "something to drink" was as necessary a "condition of thought" as Time and Space.' Casual phrases like these betray a mind of philosophic culture, but they mar the simplicity of the style. When the author is describing scenery, which he does with poetic felicity, or in his emotional and reflective passages, the style has none of these literary betrayals . . .

We know not whether George Eliot has most power over tears or laughter; but as humour is a rarer quality than pathos, we are disposed to admire his humour most. It is very genuine, and not only plays like lambent flame amid the descriptions, but animates the dialogues with dramatic life. And this leads us to notice another merit in these stories—the characters are not only true portraits, but they are living beings. Their feelings and motives are seen to be part and parcel of their natures and conditions, their talk is individual, belongs strictly to *them*, and not to the author. Hence even the little scraps of village gossip, or kitchen talk, introduced to carry on the story, have an independent life-like value. Whether the dialect is correctly or incorrectly given, we cannot say, but we are quite certain that the language is that of peasants, farmers, and servants, not the language of fiction. . . .
The work has satire, but the satire is loving; it has pathos, but the tears make human nature more beautiful; it is homely in its pictures, but they are connected with our most impassioned sensibilities and our daily

duties; it is religious, without cant or intolerance; and as Ruskin says
of a good book, 'It may contain firm assertion or stern satire, but it never
sneers coldly, nor asserts haughtily; and it always leads you to love or
reverence something with your whole heart.'

From an unsigned review of *Scenes of Clerical Life*, *The Saturday
Review*, No. 135, Vol. 5, 29 May 1858, pp. 566–7.

ELIZABETH GASKELL: 1859
Janet's Repentance

. . . I think I have a feeling that it is not worth while trying to write,
while there are such books as Adam Bede & Scenes from Clerical
Life—I set 'Janet's Repentance' above all. . . .

From a letter to Charles Eliot Norton, 25 October 1859, in J. A. V.
Chapple and A. Pollard (eds) *The Letters of Mrs Gaskell*, Manchester
University Press, 1966, p. 581.

ANONYMOUS: 1859
'Adam Bede'—A Woman's Work?

. . . The scene of the story is the village of Hayslope, as it existed before
the invasion of railroads, newspapers, and 'high' and 'low' Churchism.
The author has chosen to conceal from us the exact situation of Hayslope, by locating it in that large county, 'Loamshire', a region which
may be taken to comprise the Midland Counties . . . To anyone who has
lived in the Midland Counties, the dialect of the inhabitants of those
villages resounds as the familiar language of childhood. Whittaws
(harness-makers), gell (girl), a soft (a fool), a cade lamb (a pet lamb),
thack (thatch), thrall (a sort of table, sometimes of wood, sometimes of
brick), and many other words which we might cite from *Adam Bede*,
are in constant use at this day in the districts where, as we contend,
Hayslope and Snowfield are situated. [The word geek, used once or
twice, we suspect to be an importation from Yorkshire.]

The chief characters of the story are two journeymen carpenters and
their querulous mother; a farmer and his wife and family, including
two marriageable nieces; the rector, and the young squire of Hayslope.
The central figure, Adam Bede, is a fine stalwart, broad-chested fellow,
whose mind is as robust and firmly set as his body. His large head and
overhanging brow denote the native force, vigorous grasp, and practical
character of his intellect. He is self-sufficing, and has an unconscious
trust in himself. He contrasts strikingly with the dreamy character of
his brother Seth, whose eyebrows, we are told, had less prominence
and more repose than Adam's, and in whose forehead 'you discern the
exact contour of a coronal arch that predominates very decidedly over

the brow'. Our author did wisely in pointing out these structural
differences as the organic source of the widely differing characters of
the two men. Their mother, Lisbeth, remembered how, when a child,
'Seth 'ud allays lie i'th'cradle wi' his eyes open;' whereas 'Adam ne'er
'ud lie still a minute when he wakened.' Seth's 'glance, instead of being
keen, is confiding and benignant.' He lacks the practical element so
conspicuous in his brother; is prone to aimless musing and reverie.
You see at once that when the tide of Methodism reached to Hayslope,
he was sure to be swept along with it, while Adam kept his ground. On
one occasion, Seth, who was employed in the same workshop with his
brother, exclaimed—'There! I've finished my door to-day, anyhow!'
Amid the laughter of his fellow-workmen, he was reminded that he
had left out the panels. They ascribed his absence of mind to the influence which Methodism had got over him. But Seth himself, when
referring to the affair of the door, gave a truer account of the matter—
'It is na religion,' said he, 'as was o'fault there; it was Seth Bede, as was
allays a wool gathering chap, and religion has na cured him, the more's
the pity.' Adam is always intent on doing the duty which lies straight
before him. Seth is chiefly concerned about saving souls. On the death
of their father, who was drowned when returning home drunk, and
whom Adam had often upbraided for his thoughtless and ruinous life,
their opposite characters came out in strong relief. 'Seth's chief feeling
was awe and distress at this sudden snatching away of his father's soul;
but Adam's mind rushed back over the past in a flood of relenting and
pity'. . . .

It will be readily understood how greatly the respect and trust of the
inhabitants of Hayslope centred in Adam Bede. But, alas! his clear-
sightedness, undeviating rectitude, and unblemished life, could not
shield him from terrible mental misery. So closely are we knitted
together by the tangled web of interests and affections, that no man can
isolate himself and live his own life, undisturbed by those around him.
In Adam's case, the external forces which exerted a paramount influence
upon him were the two nieces of the Poysers, who occupied the Hall
Farm, and Captain Donnithorne, the squire of Hayslope. One of these
nieces, Hetty Sorrel, resided permanently at the Farm; the other,
Dinah Morris, paid long visits to her aunt, and was repeatedly urged to
stay with her altogether, but her duties at Snowfield constrained her to
spend much of her time there. She had 'a call' to minister to the spiritual needs of the poor miners of that barren district.

This fair young Methodist, Mr Eliot tells us, had 'a small oval face,
of a uniform transparent whiteness, with an egg-like line of cheek and
chin, a full but firm mouth, a delicate nostril, and a low perpendicular
brow, surmounted by a rising arch of parting, between smooth locks
of pale reddish hair'. Her character seems to have been a mixture of the
ecstatic spiritualism of Madame Guyon with the earnest love of souls
which shaped the life of Wesley. When young, she heard him preach;
and living at Snowfield with her aunt, who was a member of the

society, she had cause to be thankful, she said, for the privileges which she had thereby from her earliest childhood. The influence of that fervid form of Christianity on Dinah's pure, impressible, and self-forgetting nature, is admirably depicted . . . A strong sense of duty was the ruling principle both of Adam and of Dinah; their benevolent feelings were probably also equally deep and ardent; and what is more to the point, the manner of each, in carrying out their ideas and feelings, was equally practical and effective. In fact, their spiritual affinities were strong and numerous; but there were also seemingly insurmountable barriers between them . . . But besides these obstacles which prevented the natural affinities by which Adam and Dinah were related to each other from coming into action, an extraneous influence was attracting Adam with a power to which he could not but yield himself. He was on visiting terms at the Hall Farm, where Dinah's cousin, Hetty Sorrel, was budding into womanhood. To say that she was the belle of Hayslope would convey no adequate notion of her extraordinary beauty, which seems to have fascinated not only men, but women. . . . If the reader could imagine the subtle, inexpressible beauty which Hetty rejoiced in, he will easily understand that a man like Captain Donnithorne would yield himself up to its fascination, attending only so far to hide conscientious scruples as was needful in order to argue them away. And so it happened: . . . Friendless and in utter despair she expended her last resources in getting back to the neighbourhood of Stoniton, half-resolved on going to Snowfield to cast herself on Dinah, but her courage failed her: she could not expose her shame to anyone who knew her. Having become a mother in the house of a poor woman who befriended her in Stoniton, she stole away suddenly with her baby, and at length abandoned it alive in a field near the town. The child was found dead, evidence was forthcoming to prove that it was Hetty's, she was convicted of the crime with which she was charged, was condemned to death, and was only saved from this last ignominy by the commutation of her sentence to transportation for life. This naked outline of poor Hetty's history is filled in by Mr. Eliot with scenes and incidents full of intense interest; they are narrated with admirable simplicity and impressiveness, and the narrative itself is pervaded by such wisdom and charity as ought to make every reader the better for reading it.

Such are the manifold relations of human beings to each other that when a heroic deed is done, or a crime committed, all participate in the ennoblement of the hero, or in the degradation of the criminal in proportion to their nearness to the one or the other. As the goodness of the good man is fruitful of blessings to himself and to those around him, so crime results in suffering not only to the criminal, but to all connected with him. If we always bore in mind that no cause produces one effect only, but innumerable effects—the secondary one producing another, and so on in endless succession—how great and solemn should we feel our responsibilities, how we should shrink from wrong! Captain Donnithorne acted as if he thought consequences could be confirmed within the circle of the actors, whereas he not only involved Hetty in the tragic fate just mentioned, but plunged Adam Bede, the Poysers and their relatives and friends, into misery which they had no share in causing, and which they were powerless to avert. How nature exacts security from every man for the good conduct of his neighbour, how she punishes the innocent with the guilty, how—to use Mr. Eliot's expression —'the bitter waters spread,' is strikingly illustrated in this Hayslope History. It also clearly shows, what indeed is but another side of the same truth, that strictly speaking no sin can be atoned for—no wrong righted. This we take to be the chief moral of the story, a moral which Adam Bede seems to have drawn early from his own experience, and which by long and intense suffering on account of Hetty he abundantly confirmed. . . .

But though wrong once done can never be undone, and though its consequences can never be effaced, there often grows, thank God! out of the sorrow that wrong induces a hallowing influence, which enlarges our affections, gives depth and tenderness to our sympathies, and fills us with charity towards the errors and weaknesses of our fellows, to whom we seem more nearly related than before, and whose lives and actions we can now estimate more justly.

How Adam's pain was gradually transformed into sympathy, how affection and friendship became more precious to him than they used to be, and how he clung more closely to his mother and to Seth, and had unspeakable satisfaction in the sight or imagination of any small addition to their happiness, is beautifully sketched. Hopes radiant with joy, such as those which Hetty had inspired in him, were, he imagined, extinct; love, he thought, could never be anything to him but a living memory—a limb lopped off but not gone from consciousness, and *thus* he worked on, his work continuing as it had always been, a part of his religion; for 'from very early days he saw clearly that good carpentry was God's will—was that form of God's will that most immediately concerned him.' But though Adam was unconscious of it, the spirit of love was creating a new life in him, hidden as yet beneath the sorrowful experiences of the past, but destined soon to burst forth again, fruitful of serene and lasting happiness. . . .

Mrs. Poyster is one of the most original characters Mr. Eliot has portrayed. Some faint ideas of her sterling common sense, piercing insight, and caustic humour, may be obtained from the few of her sayings that can be isolated from the context, but a just conception of her is only to be had by studying her in her everyday life as mistress of the Hall Farm. We commend her judicious observations on marriage to all whom they may concern:

'Ah,' she would say, 'It's all very fine having a ready-made rich man, but may-happen he'll be a ready-made fool, and it's no use filling your pocket full of money if you've got a hole in the corner. It'll do you no good to sit in a spring-cart o' your own, if you've got a soft to drive you; he'll soon turn you over into the ditch. I allays said I'd never marry a man as had got no brains; for where's the use of a woman having brains of her own if she's tackled to a geek as everybody's a laughing at? She might as well dress herself fine to sit back'ards on a donkey.'

Mrs Poyser's objection to late marriages is perhaps equally worthy of attention:

'I am no friend', said Mr. Poyser, 'to young fellows a-marr'ing afore they know the differences atween a crab an' a apple; but they may wait o'er long.' 'To be sure,' replied his wife, 'If you go past your dinner-time, there'll be little relish o' your meat. You turn it o'er and o'er an' o'er wi' your fork, an' don't eat it after all. You find fault wi' your meat, and the fault's all i' your own stomach.'

The existence of old bachelors Mrs. Poyser accounted for by the following ingenious theory:

'Yes,' said she, 'I know what the men like—a poor soft, as 'ud simper at 'em, like the pictur' o' the sun, whether they did right or wrong, and say thank you for a kick, and pretend she didna know which end she stood uppermost till her husband told her. That's what a man wants in a wife mostly; he wants to make sure o' one fool as 'll tell him he's wise. But there's some men can do without that—they think so much o' themselves a'ready; an' that's how it is there's old bachelors.'

Her estimate of Mr. Craig, Squire Donnithorne's gardener, who was perhaps somewhat given to *over*-estimate himself [he was a bachelor] is highly characteristic:

'For my part I think he's welly like a cock as thinks the sun rose o' purpose to hear him crow.'. . .

We have seldom read a book in which we could find so few faults as are detectable in *Adam Bede*. There is perhaps a little too much minute description and detail here and there, especially in the account of the harvest supper. This, however, is a fault leaning to virtue's side. Dutch pictures are always valuable, and their faithful realism is infinitely preferable to those products of 'high art', in which all individuality of character is merged into vague, expressionless, and generalized human faces, evincing no particular attribute, and presumed therefore to comprehend all. The introduction of the supernatural incident on the night when Thias Bede was drowned is, in our opinion, a disfigurement. We doubt the artistic fidelity of making Captain Donnithorne gallop up the street of Stoniton with a reprieve in his hand at the very time when Hetty is actually on her way to the scaffold: this seems to us in the style of a dramatic trick. We think, too, that the history is brought to a close too abruptly. The reader longs to know somewhat of the fate of Hetty during those dreary years of transportation, as well as the circumstances of her death. It would also be a satisfaction to him to be informed of the chief events of Captain Donnithorne's life after his return to Hayslope. But we suppose the author wrote under the inexorable condition of filling three volumes of the stereotyped size, and of not exceeding them. If so, he has doubtless exercised a wise discretion in determining what to publish and what to withhold.

We speak of the author as of the masculine gender, but the delicate appreciation of feminine feeling conveyed in this question—'What woman was ever satisfied with apparent neglect, even when she knows it is the mask of love?' would alone suffice to make us sceptical as to whether *George Eliot* ever wrote it. Not this sentence only, however, but many scattered throughout the work display such an acute and subtle perception and delineation of the affections and of the countless ways in which they manage to express themselves while eluding even the most vigilant of *man*-kind, that we are forced over and over again to doubt whether, after all, George Eliot is a real person. . . .

A character built up from the firm foundations of native sagacity and an indomitable sense of justice as is that of Adam Bede, or developed from the loose material constituting the good-intentioned, but weak, vacillating, and self-indulgent mind of Captain Donnithorne, or moulded and directed by an informing and ever-present influence— an unfaltering religious faith, as was Dinah's, is, in our opinion, far more easy to understand and describe, than it is to track the devious course of a wayward creature like Hetty throughout the latter part of her career. The more completely a mind is directed by unreasoning impulses and seeming caprice, the more difficult it becomes to imagine its probable action under extraordinary circumstances, and the more entirely is the artist compelled to trust his instinct or genius for guidance. This trust is manifest to us in the description of the poor, stricken, helpless Hetty during her journey to Windsor, of her fitful, aimless wanderings and return to Stoniton, of her struggles between her impulses to drown herself and her intense horror of death, of the abandonment of her child, her mental attitude during her trial, and especially the last scene in prison, when her death-like impenetrability is at length overcome by Dinah's deep and effective sympathy.

But the hypothesis that the book is written by a woman is beset with even greater difficulties than is the belief in George Eliot. Few perhaps have greater faith in woman, and in what she may accomplish than we have; but how many woman are there of this generation who combine the breadth, depth, and justness of thought, the genuine catholic spirit of religion—freed from all verbal formulae, the vigorous imagination which fashions its creations with the unity and minute accuracy of detail that belongs to organic growths, the wit, humour, and rich poetic feeling, and the admirable simplicity and lucidity of exposition, which distinguish the author of *Adam Bede*. . . .

From an unsigned review of *Adam Bede*, *The Westminster Review*,
Vol. 71, April 1859, pp. 486–512 (488–90, 493–5, 498–9, 506–7,
510–12).

LEO TOLSTOY: 1898
Religious Art: 'Adam Bede'

... religious art—transmitting both positive feeling of love of God and
one's neighbour, and negative feelings of indignation and horror at the
violation of love—manifests itself chiefly in the form of words. . . . If I
were asked to give modern examples . . . then . . . I should name . . . the
novels and stories of Dickens . . . and others—*Uncle Tom's Cabin*;
Dostoevski's works—especially his *Memoirs from the House of Death*—
and *Adam Bede*. . . .

From *What is Art?* in Aylmer Maude (tr.) *The Works of Tolstoy*.
Tolstoy Centenery Edition Vol. 18, Oxford, 1929–37, pp. 241–2.

W. LUCAS COLLINS: 1860
The Mill on the Floss

... We need no title-page to inform us that the *Mill on the Floss* is by
the author of *Adam Bede*. It is scarcely possible that it should meet
with a warmer welcome than its predecessor; it would be an ungrateful
comparison to say that it deserves it. Yet if we are to treat it merely as a
novel, in point of dramatic interest it is incontestably superior. There is
the same keen insight into nature, the same truth and force of description, the same bright and graceful humour; but the story, which in *Adam
Bede* was subordinate to the other attractions of the book, is here one of
its greatest charms. As before, the personages whom we are to accompany through some of their life-struggles are very carefully introduced to us at the outset, and we have to make their acquaintance
thoroughly before the story is suffered to proceed; but the result is
that we know them so intimately that they keep fast hold of our sympathies to the end. And the interest, when once fairly started, though not
rapid, never flags. It is not of that intense and exciting kind which
tempts the reader, unable to finish at a sitting, to turn over the last
half-volume 'to see the end'; but we lay the book aside thoughtfully,
content to feel that there is so much enjoyment still behind. . . .

The actors in the story are of the middle class—what we may call the
lower middle class—even more exclusively than in *Adam Bede.* There
is not a full-bred gentleman or lady (in the conventional sense of the
words) in the whole of the three volumes; for even Mr. Stephen Guest,
the rich young banker, must be supposed to have risen from the ranks.
. . . It is from that worst aspect of the money-making middle class—
their narrow-minded complacent selfishness, their money-worship,

their petty schemes and jealousies—that much, not only of the comedy, but even of the tragedy, of the *Mill on the Floss* is drawn. Mr Tulliver himself, indeed, is rather of the country-farmer type; but his wife's family, the Dodsons—who are richer people, and consider Mrs. Tulliver's a poor match—have all the selfish hardness which the successful pursuit of small gains breeds in their class—their very virtues are mean. . . .

Each figure is filled in by a series of minute touches, which are really the perfection of art; while the conversation between the speakers seems to the reader to flow as easily and readily as though it had been taken down from actual life. In this point, too, the present book seems to us superior to *Adam Bede*; exquisite as the dialogue was there, it sometimes bore the marks of the artist's hand; the reader felt, from time to time, that he was listening to the writer in his study—not to the speakers in the carpenter's shop. We hope the whole explanation does not lie in the humiliating truth, that the Gleggs and the Pullets represent such a much larger portion of the world around us than Seth or Adam.

So very natural, indeed, and therefore so very disagreeable, are these relations of Mrs. Tulliver's, that we should feel we had too much of their company—that, like pictures of diseased organs in medical books, they were too accurately truthful to be pleasant—but that they are wholesomely relieved by two of the very best portraits of child-life that have ever been drawn. Not that Tom and Maggie, the children of Dorlcote Mill, are perfect ideals of any kind. They are quite different from those happy families of wingless cherubs that we hear of occasionally (in books), or those very disagreeable little girls and boys whom we also read of, and who are occasionally introduced to our admiration by fond parents. These are two real children, compounds of flesh and spirit, good and evil. They merely say and do what children have said and done, with variations, a thousand times over, and yet it all reads to us fresh and new. Why is it so delightful to read what we have all known and felt so well already? Is it a confirmation of the assertion which some philosophers have hazarded, that all knowledge is nothing more than recollection? We have neither space nor inclination to discuss the principle; the fact remains. Tom and Maggie Tulliver delight us, because they say and do nothing more or less than either we remember to have said and done when children ourselves, or have known other children say and do. . . .

The moral characteristics of the two children differ as widely as their physical. Tom never does any wrong that he is not prepared to justify in some way to his own conscience—'I'd do just the same again,' is his usual mode of viewing his past actions; while poor Maggie is 'always wishing she had done something different'. 'A bitter sense of the irrevocable' is an 'almost everyday experience of her small soul.' She 'rushes to her deeds with passionate impulse, and then sees not only their consequences, but what would have happened if they had not been done, with all the detail and exaggerated circumstance of an active imagination.' This faculty of hers implies, of course, a love of books, her brother Tom's abhorrence; of books of all kinds, some most unusual in the catalogue of a little girl's library—including even Defoe's *History of the Devil*, by an enthusiastic extempore lecture upon which subject she very much alarms and astonishes her father and his friend the auctioneer as they sit over their brandy-and-water. She is a strangely imaginative child in many ways; she can tell stories, at a moment's notice, for her own and her companions' amusement, of 'all the live things they come upon by accident'; can invent biographies for the toads in whom Tom takes a lively interest (being 'one of those boys who are fond of animals—fond, that is, of throwing stones at them'); if an earwig hurries across their path, she has its private history all ready—'how Mrs. Earwig had a wash at home, and one of her children had fallen into the hot copper, for which reason she was running so fast to fetch the doctor'—until Tom, stern and contemptuous, sets his foot upon the unlucky subject, and so hurries the catastrophe. But her character is best shown in her solitary pursuits in the great attic under the high-pitched roof at home. . . . Not that Margaret Tulliver occupies the stage too exclusively. Here, as in the former work, the artist has studied carefully the harmonies of colour. The complement to this impulsive, imaginative, vigorous, but yielding nature is put in with equal care, and perhaps with equal success. The brother—with his resolute will, hard self-reliance, narrow inflexible justice, honest and true, but with only that 'hard rind of truth, which is discerned by unsympathetic minds'—is probably as true to nature, and even more original in fiction, than the sister, who absorbs the larger share of our sympathies. He too has his trials and his struggles. If we hear less of them, it is only because, with a manful determination, he buries them in his own breast. If they fail to interest us, that may be not the hero's fault, but ours.

. . . In the *Mill on The Floss* none of the characters approach perfection; the heroine as little as any; yet we will venture to assert that Maggie's passionate and rebellious weakness has more interest for us, however undeservedly, than Adam's enduring strength. The true heroic struggles, which are silent and successful, are a spectacle for gods, not men. The indications of weakness and peril must be patent, to gain any deep sympathy from mortal lookers-on.

The moral of these volumes is not obtrusive. The reader will probably draw it for himself according as he is predisposed. But he will gather nothing but good from it, read it how he will. On one point only, we think, the writer has shown an undue severity—though, even here, it is a severity in the cause of charity. The little provincial world of St. Ogg's is of course highly censorious, has little of that charity that thinks no evil, and punishes, with all the emphasis of such a small Rhadamanthus, an aberration from the recognized proprieties. In several pages of brilliant sarcasm, we are drawn to infer that the world of St. Ogg's is very mean and wrong. But we have been watching the struggle of which St. Ogg's sees only the *apparent* end. It is quite true that the world judges harshly and uncharitably often, because it judges from appearances and from results; it belongs to a higher Power to look at the heart and the motives. If society were to claim this 'discerning of spirits', its judgements would be erroneous oftener still, and infinitely more mischievous than now. In the present instance, Dr. Kenn, the rector, alone judges by a larger and more charitable standard. He braves in this quarrel—not quite successfully—public opinion at St. Ogg's. Dr. Kenn was right—grandly, heroically right; does it follow so certainly that society at St. Ogg's was wrong? That Higher Authority whose example he pleads, is indeed the great court of appeal from every human judgement. Even he could do, as the recognized exponent of that Authority, what others could scarcely venture upon. For society cannot shift its landmarks; they may be arbitrary, but they are well known; it is at our peril if of our own will, to our sad cost if by force of circumstances, we overstep them. For there is a large floating mass of weak morality from which such definite restrictions are the best safe-guard. Society sits as a court of law, and gives judgement according to its written statutes; in the main it does justice. Those on whom it presses hardly—and they are many—must be content with that other Court of last appeal. If 'their own hearts condemn them not,' they may find their judgement reversed there.

But we have closed the book. Only in striving to right what seems a wrong, does even satire in these hands wear its common bitterness. Alike in power, but how very different in its use, is George Eliot in this point from another of our great novelists; he, with the same keen perception, and knowledge of the universal disease, slashes remorselessly through the fair skin, and shows us, as with a fierce professional satisfaction, the lurking evil within; here we watch a hand not less steady or less skilful, which, if it cuts deeply through the cancerous growth, does so in confidence that there is wholesome life beneath. After all the hard words of truth dealt against our neighbours on the Floss side, it is as if the author—like Maggie in the story—could not part even from the most narrow-minded of them without a word of forgive-ness. Mr. and Mrs. Stelling (with the last half-year's bills never likely to be paid) dismiss poor Tom with a blessing and a basket; even Lawyer Wakem was doing something which he meant for kindness, when we saw him last; and aunt Clegg—that Dodson of Dodsons—when cir-cumstances occur which are quite out of line of the Dodson experience, and to which the rules of the Dodson religion no longer apply—astonishes the reader as much as the world at St. Ogg's. It is remarkable, indeed, that neither here nor in *Adam Bede* are any of the characters esteemed so evil in their author's sight, as to stand in need of the usual penalties of poetic retribution.

"Retribution may come from any voice: the hardest, cruellest, most imbruted urchin at the street-corner can inflict it: surely help

and pity are rarer things—more needful for the righteous to bestow. . . .

From an unsigned review, *Blackwood's Edinburgh Magazine*, Vol. 87,
May 1860, pp. 611–23, (611–16, 621–3).

SIR EDWARD BULWER-LYTTON: 1860
Unheroic Maggie

. . . the error . . . of her whole position towards Stephen. It may be
quite natural that she should take that liking to him, but it is a position
at variance with all that had before been Heroic about her [i.e. Maggie
Tulliver]. The *indulgence* of such a sentiment for the affianced of a
friend under whose roof she was, was a treachery and a meanness
according to the Ethics of Art, and nothing can afterwards lift the
character into the same hold on us. The refusal to marry Stephen fails
to do so. . . .

From a letter to Blackwood, 4 May 1860, in *The George Eliot Letters*,
Vol. 3. p. 317, fn. 9, from a letter in National Library of Scotland.

JOHN RUSKIN: 1881
The Sweepings out of a Pentonville Omnibus

. . . in the railway novel, interest is obtained with the vulgar reader for
the vilest character, because the author describes carefully to his
recognition the blotches, burrs and pimples in which the paltry nature
resembles his own. *The Mill on the Floss* is perhaps the most striking
extent of this study of cutaneous disease. There is not a single person
in the book of the smallest importance to anybody in the world but
themselves, or whose qualities deserved so much as a line of printer's
type in their description. There is no girl alive, fairly clever, half
educated, and unluckily related, whose life has not at least as much in
it as Maggie's, to be described and to be pitied. Tom is a clumsy and
cruel lout, with the making of better things in him (and the same may
be said of nearly every Englishman at present smoking and elbowing
his way through the ugly world his blunders have contributed to the
making of); while the rest of the characters are simply the sweepings
out of a Pentonville omnibus. . . .

From 'Fiction, Fair and Foul', *Nineteenth Century*, Vol. 10, No. 56,
October 1881, pp. 516–31. Reprinted in E. T. Cook and A. Wedder-
burn (eds), *The Works of John Ruskin*, Vol. 33, pp. 376–7.

ANONYMOUS: 1861
Silas Marner, the Weaver of Raveloe

It is a great gain, because full of promise to her readers, that the last of George's Eliot's works is undoubtedly the finest, the stream of thought runs clearer, the structure of the story is more compact, while the philosophical insight is deeper and more penetrating than in any of her former productions. It has been said that *Silas Marner* is deficient in interest, but the only element in which it can be called wanting is that which is supplied by the vulgar excitement of exceptional circumstances or of abnormal characters. In *Silas Marner*, the dead level and dry bones of English country life fifty years since, are illuminated and vivified by a power of sympathetic insight which is one of the rarest of intellectual gifts. There is nothing so difficult to a cultivated intellect as to enter into the mental states of the ignorant and uninformed, it is an accomplishment of genius alone, the minutest analysis, and the most comprehensive inductions are but tools and helps in such a task. In the progress towards clear conceptions of any kind, the vestiges of the confused notions they replace are trodden out, the memory of our first feeble intellectual life is as irrecoverable and obscure as that of our physical birth. Insight into the past conditions even of our own minds, is one of the rarest acquisitions of reflection; and the difficulty of attaining such insight when times and men foreign to ourselves are concerned is so great, that it is only within the last generation that even history has aspired to do more than chronicle the events of each succeeding year.

Heretofore novelists have either relied on an interesting and well-constructed tale, or on the gradual and skilful development of a well-considered plot, or on unexpected solutions of prepared difficulties; and when this has been the case the study of character has generally been weak and incomplete; or they have seized upon some particular type of character the growth of which they wish to display, and this in case the circumstances in which the hero or heroine is placed are generally forced and unnatural, being neglected as subordinate to the main purpose of the author. The most remarkable peculiarity and distinguishing excellence of *Silas Marner* is the complete correlation between the characters and their circumstances; the actors in this story come before us like the flowers of their own fields, native to the soil and varying with each constituent of the earth from which they spring, with every difference that is implied in defective or excessive nutriment, but yet no more the creatures of blind chance, each asserting his own individuality after his kind, and none over-stepping the possibilities of culture furnished by such a world-forgotten village as Raveloe. It is impossible to dissociate any of the characters from the village in which they were born and bred—they form an organic whole with Raveloe; they are not connected with it by any external, or even humorous bands, but by vital threads that will not bear disruption. The stranger

Silas is at last assimilated by the little society, and only truly lives when the process has been completed. Nothing can be more profound than this picture of the manner in which all human beings are influenced by their environment, the consequence of this most wonderful fitness between the characters and the scene of their life, is that on laying down the book we do not dwell upon Silas Marner or Godfrey Cass or Dolly Winthrop, or any particular character, but are forced to embrace them all with all their restricted country life; nothing short of all Raveloe satisfies the memory; there is no episode that can be detached from the story, no character than can be spared, much less conceived other than it shows itself; there is about them all a certain absoluteness like that which characterizes the works of nature.

In her former works the author has taken a more or less critical position over against society; in the present one, though criticism cannot sleep in such an intellect, she appreciates more fully the strange compensations which accompany incomplete states of development, and brings out, without express statement, that conclusion which has so often stood at the commencement of many a feeble sermon, that there is but little connexion after all between a high moral character and clear conceptions of morality.

The profound insight with which the seed of retribution is shown shrouded in every act, and the intimate fitness which this retribution assumes in her hands is beyond praise; truth calls not for praise, but demands acknowledgment. Novels claim to illustrate the instructiveness of life; but this instructiveness, however, is in direct proportion to the truth of the picture, and the light thrown on it by the author. Mostly it is the case that where the reflections are true and just, the situations are exceptional, or where the circumstances are those of every-day life, the remarks on them are weak, trivial, or obvious. Of *Silas Marner* it is impossible to say which is most admirable, the vivid painting of life itself, or the profound remarks on the progress of that life; nor is this all, the kindly humour which glows through every judgment is as conciliating as the verdict is convincing, and the more so as the author shows no foregone purpose in the construction of the fable, but leaves it to bear its own fruit. It not so much directly instructs as adds to the experience of its readers, and like life itself adds to it in proportion to their power of understanding the results it offers. There is no single feature of this novel which will surprise those who are acquainted with the former works of the author, their greatest beauties are to be found in this; the objections which have been taken to the incompleteness and insufficiency of Captain Donnithorne and Stephen Guest, are here met by the best of all possible answers in the full and masterly treatment of the character of Godfrey Cass; the profound truth and delicate dis-crimination evinced in the delineation of this character are but too apt to be overlooked; it is one of those portraits which gain upon you the more you look at it, and which you leave with the feeling that no art could improve. A somewhat objectionable use of physiological images which certainly disfigures some few pages of the *Mill on the Floss*, is no longer recognizable, but the author's talent, like some fine crystal, assuming its definite form, has here purged out of its symmetrical structure all impurities and foreign substances. . . .

From an unsigned review, *The Westminster Review*, Vol. 76, July 1861, pp. 280–2.

HENRY JAMES: 1866
Romola

. . . I have come to the end of my space without speaking of *Romola*, which, as the most important of George Eliot's works, I had kept in reserve. I have only room to say that on the whole I think it is decidedly the most important,—not the most entertaining nor the most readable, but the one in which the largest things are attempted and grasped. The figure of Savonarola, subordinate though it is, is a figure on a larger scale then any which George Eliot has elsewhere undertaken; and in the career of Tito Melema there is a fuller representation of the development of a character. Considerable as are our author's qualities as an artist, and largely as they are displayed in *Romola*, the book strikes me less as a work of art than as a work of morals. Like all of George Eliot's works, its dramatic construction is feeble; the story drags and halts, the setting is too large for the picture; but I remember that, the first time I read it, I declared to myself that much should be forgiven it for the sake of its generous feeling and its elevated morality. I still recognize this latter fact, but I think I find it more on a level than I at first found it with the artistic conditions of the book. 'Our deeds determine us', George Eliot says somewhere in *Adam Bede*, 'as much as we determine our deeds.' This is the moral lesson of *Romola*. A man has no associate so intimate as his own character, his own career,—his present and his past; and if he builds up his career of timid and base actions, they cling to him like evil companions, to sophisticate, to corrupt, and to damn him. As in Maggie Tulliver we had a picture of the elevation of the moral tone by honesty and generosity, so that when the mind found itself face to face with the need for a strong muscular effort, it was competent to perform it; so in Tito we have a picture of that depression of the moral tone by falsity and self-indulgence, which gradually evokes on every side of the subject some implacable claim, to be avoided or propitiated. At last all his unpaid debts join issue before him, and he finds the path of life a hideous blind alley. Can any argument be more plain? Can any lesson be more salutary? 'Under every guilty secret,' writes the author, with her usual felicity, 'there is a hidden brood of guilty wishes, whose unwholesome, infecting life is cherished by the darkness. The contaminating effect of deeds often lies less in the commission than in the consequent adjustment of our desires,—the enlistment of self-interest on the side of falsity; as, on the other hand, the purifying influence of public confession springs from the fact, that by it the hope in lies is forever swept away, *and the soul recovers the noble attitude of simplicity*'. And again: 'Tito was experiencing that inexorable law of human souls, that we prepare ourselves for sudden deeds by the reiterated choice of good or evil that gradually determines character.' Somewhere else I think she says, in purport, that our deeds are like our children; we beget them, and rear them and cherish them, and they grow up and turn against us and misuse us. The fact that has led me to a belief in the fundamental equality between the worth of *Romola* as a moral argument and its value as a work of art, is the fact that in each character it seems to me essentially prosaic. The excellence both of the spirit and of the execution of the book is emphatically an obvious excellence. They make no demand upon the imagination of the reader. It is true of both of them that he who runs may read them. It may excite surprise that I should intimate that George Eliot is deficient in imagination; but I believe that I am right in so doing. Very readable novels have been written without imagination; and as compared with writers who, like Mr. Trollope, are totally destitute of the faculty, George Eliot may be said to be richly endowed with it. But as compared with writers whom we are tempted to call decidedly imaginative, she must, in my opinion, content herself with the very solid distinction of being exclusively an observer. In confirmation of this I would suggest a comparison of those chapters in *Adam Bede* which treat of Hetty's flight and wanderings, and those of Miss Bronte's *Jane Eyre* which describe the heroine's escape from Rochester's house and subsequent perambulations. The former are throughout admirable prose; the latter are in portions very good poetry. . . .

From 'The Novels of George Eliot', *Atlantic Monthly*, Vol. 18, October 1866, pp. 479–92 (490–2).

ROBERT BROWNING: 1863
Disappointment

. . . I told you what I thought of the *two* first volumes of *Romola* as honestly, I add now that I was much disappointed in the third and last: there was too much dwelling on the delinquencies of the Greek after he had been done for, and might have been done with, as a pure and perfect rascal—while the great interests, Savonarola and the Republic, which I expected would absorb attention and pay for the previous minutenesses, dwindled strangely. My impression of the great style and high tone remain, of course,—but, as a work of art, I want much. Other people like it—I heard Gladstone loud in its praise the other day at dinner. . . .

From a letter to Isabella Blagden, 19 November 1863, in Edward C. McAleer (ed.) *Dearest Isa: Robert Browning's Letters to Isabella Blagden*, Austin, Texas, University of Texas Press, 1951, p. 178.

FRANCIS TURNER PALGRAVE: 1886
George Eliot's Limitations

. . . Have read through *Romola* after many years. A sense of gloom and heaviness and anatomical power remains with all the ability and knowledge shown; one hardly ever escapes the feeling that it is all *mosaic-work*, not brushwork, all put together, little grown. Much of the traits of the main characters are told us, not shown before us. . . . The whole narrative is infected and narrowed by the poison of suppressed Calvinism. . . .

From G. Palgrave, *Francis Turner Palgrave: the Journals and Memorials of His Life*, Longmans, 1899, *Journal*, May 1886, p. 201.

A. G. SEDGEWICK: 1886
Felix Holt, the Radical

There are one or two hints in *Romola* and *Felix Holt* that the author in writing them had a definite dramatic aim, which would not be satisfied with works properly inartistic. The bill-sticking scene in *Felix Holt*, and the chapter called 'A Florentine Joke' in *Romola*, are easier to account for on the supposition of a design to heighten the unity and interest of the plot by contrast, than on the grounds of a purely naturalistic development of the story. And there are other hints at the same thing, rather to be found in the general tone of George Eliot's later books, than in any marked incidents or relations of incidents. But as she has never distinctly said that this was her ambition, and as it is possible to explain everything in her books in another way, it is much better to look at such excellent novels from the simplest point of view, and to leave to the French the aesthetic discussion of her works; for they still do such criticism far better than we, and are troubled less than we by other considerations. When George Eliot comes to write the drama which is perhaps foreshadowed in the verses scattered through *Felix Holt*, then it will be time enough to talk of her as a dramatic author. But while we still refuse to bring this kind of criticism to bear upon Thackeray and Dickens, let us enjoy her rare qualities also, without inquiring how it is that she is not what perhaps she never meant to be.

From the time when the interesting *Scenes of Clerical Life* were published down to the issue of *Felix Holt*, George Eliot has the great merit of being true to herself. Her last novel shows the distinctive marks of the first, the vigour of style, the incisiveness of thought, the truth to nature. The corruption which a life of fiction-writing, like a life of politics, is apt to produce, has not been able to dull her moral sense, nor to rust the keenness of her sympathy for the sorrows and joys of men and women. Even the wearing effects of time she shows but little. She has neither become a cynic, nor a humorist, nor coarse, but still keeps in the path of realistic art, studying the roadside nature, and satisfied with it. She continues to receive the great reward which every true realist longs for, that she is true to nature without degenerating to the commonplace, and the old blame, that they have not enough of the ideal, which they covet too. . . .

It is sufficiently original, and at the same time familiar, to mark it as akin to *The Mill on The Floss* and *Romola* and the *Scenes of Clerical Life*. There is the old doubt whether the forces of nature are not stronger than we, and the old faith in morality; there is the same thoughtfulness, and the same individual point of view. The Durfey-Transomes consist of Mrs. Transome, old Mr. Transome, imbecile and despised by his wife, and a son Harold, who, having made a fortune in the East, returns, a widower with a little boy, to England, where his mother has been anxiously longing for him for years. Mrs. Transome is by nature and position an aristocrat, tied by her feelings and her property to Tory Principles. She looks to her son as to someone who is to soothe the sorrow of her declining life by sympathy and affection. He returns, a good-humoured, facile, selfish man, taking an Oriental view of women, and desiring to enforce upon his mother the necessity of her sitting on cushions and dressing in silks, while he manages the estate. In almost their first interview he shocks her by announcing that he is going to stand for Parliament as a Radical. These two characters give the author the opportunity which in *Romola* and *The Mill on the Floss* was used with such effect, of bringing into daily collision a man and woman whose natures are so utterly opposed to each other that no necessity of circumstance can ever make their lives sympathetic. Just as Tom and poor Maggie Tulliver could never be brother and sister, as Tito and Romola could never be husband and wife, so Mrs. Transome and Harold can never be mother and son. Harold is something of an English Tito, with the same selfish love of ease, the same ambition, and the same want of principle, except that he has that sense of honour and tradition which amount in England to principle, and which give a stimulus to effort very different from any which an entirely non-moral person like Hetty or Tito could have. Indeed, it will not do to push such an analogy too far, for no one is more cautious than George Eliot not to repeat herself.

In the little village of Treby, an old Dissenting minister named Rufus Lyon, abstracted from this world, and living among theories of doctrine, memories of a past unknown to his congregation, and the works of benevolence, lives with his daughter Esther. In the charming character of this girl the interest of the story centres. Her delicate, sensitive nature is shocked at the coarse prose of life, and she retires into her father's library to read Byron. The first few traits of her character excite the attention, as every imperfect, impulsive woman that George Eliot draws, from Janet Dempster to this Esther Lyon, is sure to do. To modify her, to bring out her true strength, a man must be introduced whose love of the real shall crystallize her sentiments into true idealism, and

in Felix Holt such a man is found. Every one who reads knows enough of
Felix Holt, the hater of shams and cravats, to have a clear opinion of
his character. He is a wonderfully drawn man, and in the drawing of
such people is shown the unusual clearness of the author's sight. But
though her sight is never dim, her greatest power is not shown either in
Bartle Massey, or in this radical lover of Esther's. The passions and
emotions of women, or of men who have a good deal of the woman in
them, she feels, but the same passions and emotions in thoroughly
masculine men she only understands. To go no further, for instance,
than this very book, Felix Holt, consistent and natural as he is, is not so
good as a whole as Harold Transome. Harold is a masculine man, a
man of ambition, and selfish; but there is a shade of womanly delicacy
about him, which at once makes him at home in the story. Felix Holt
seems too often sent there as a representative man, and bound like all
delegates to constrained action. He stands for masculinity, as his great-
grandfather, Bartle Massey, did in another way, and masculine he must
always be; but be he ever so masculine, we feel that George Eliot is
always feminine. Such characters are often better with her in the background than in the front, as in the slight allusion to Tom Tulliver's
unhappy love for Lucy Deane, throwing a light over his whole past and
future life, there is more poetry and effectiveness than if the hint had
been boldly developed. Tito, Arthur Donnithorne, Adam Bede, are all
men who combine with distinctly masculine natures womanly feelings
that make them much more striking characters in their different
positions than it is possible for Felix Holt to be. There is no wonder that
this should be so in a writer who unites so much manly force with
feminine sensibility. When this union is allowed to exist, there is true
power, as in the best parts of her style, in characters like Harold
Transome, in the mingled strength and sensitiveness of her thoughts;
but where the union is broken, the parts have less value by themselves.
The political dinner at Treby is by no means a success, partly because
there is not enough humour to make it entertaining, but principally
because, with all her love of alehouses and street scenes, she is not
dramatically at home in them. She can analyse and describe the
character of Mrs. Nolan, or put cleverly together scenes in a barber's
shop, with the truth of an accomplished critic, but feeling is out of the
question. In Maggie Tulliver there is the tenderness of a woman describing her sister, and the strength which bridges for tenderness the
quagmire of debility. Not that Felix Holt does many things which he
ought not to have done, and leaves undone many things which he ought
to have done, but that he is the product of the understanding; such a
character as Maggie shows the union of comprehension and feeling.

    If we are to have a seduction in a novel, the interests of morality and
art will not soon find a better combination of their requirements than in
the unhappy consequences of Mrs. Transome's error. This miserable
woman, full of remorse, without penitence, tied to an imbecile husband,
slighted by a son whose affection she longs for to soften her sorrow,

insulted by her former lover with a proposition that she may save him
by revealing her shame to her son, stands as an example of the always
deepening shadows that the evil deed throws over life. Her story offers
the same inducements to sin that the sinking vessel and the cries of the
drowning offer to shipwreck. The moral in these novels is not obtruded,
any more than it is by nature. To those who are entirely deaf, *Felix
Holt* will seem not much more than a curious and interesting story;
those who can hear when shouted to will perhaps ask why the moral is
not introduced to them; but among those who have acquired a habit of
listening, it will be the more pleasing that a book so full of thought and
the lessons which teach themselves should have been written without
morbid sentiment or offensive didacticism. In a dramatic point of view,
the vague allusions of the early chapters to a past offence, the deepening
gloom of Mrs. Transome's life, the sure approach of a disclosure, and
the pagan affection of her servant, have a power which its owner too
acutely feels to use any rhetoric or artificial flourish. The incidents of
this part of the novel, and the character of the chief person, give an
opportunity for just that masculine delicacy in stating, hinting, and in
silence which marks George Eliot's greatest successes.

But it must be confessed that the plot of *Felix Holt*, like that of
Romola, marches a little slowly. We feel that the omission of a good
deal would do no injury to the interest of the story. The boy's education
which the author has been said to have received, acting upon a mind
naturally turned toward learning and research, has made her fond of
many things which the novels of women are not apt to show familiarity
with. In this one there is enough of law and politics, as in *Romola* of
history, to show great study and care; but in both cases they are made
too prominent. These studies of the past, which no novelist of the past
can make too careful, are valuable as a means; the public, which only
cares for a novel as a novel, is willing to justify the laboriousness of
such means only if it is kept out of sight. It is a pleasure-loving public,
the novel-reading one, and turns from law and history and politics
and trade to hear the story of life. When it is so generous, it is nearly a
shame to thrust it back into the ruts. This learning and research, too,
appear to have their effect on a style which at the beginning was simple
and direct, but has by the least alteration in the world become slightly
indirect and tortuous. Ideas which in the *Scenes of Clerical Life* would
have been expressed with perfect clearness are in *Felix Holt* now and
then enveloped in syllables that coil themselves about the thought
with dangerous, snake-like facility. It is seldom that this tendency
shows clearly; but there is just enough to make us regret its presence,
and to excuse a suggestion that, wherever an author goes, her style
should sun itself in the warm light of human nature, and not shiver in
the cold chambers of law and metaphysics. . . .

But an odder thing in George Eliot than any attempts of such a kind
is that she should so often have called in the assistance of Dickens. If
there was one thing in the world that seemed certain, it was that she

would not, could not, imitate, yet constantly she has imitated Dickens. There was a quaint form of humour that he introduced, and of which every one has now a large supply in hand, both for purposes of conversation and for writing, which enveloped familiar ideas, the more familiar the idea the better, in a suave, elaborate diction, which could give an absurd look to anything. It delighted him to pay out his thoughts with grandiose detail and meaningless circumlocution, and to feel the surprise of those who grasped the end to find that they had hold of spool cotton, instead of an electric cable. This manner has grown a little monotonous, even in his hands, and has been trodden to death by so many others' feet, that there seems no reason why so cautious an analyzer as George Eliot should have fallen into it. That she should have done so is one of the highest triumphs of Dickens. It was a stern literary fate that forced a person so rich in expression into copying the peculiarities, of all others, which had been hackneyed by every crumb-eater who needed out-door relief. . . .

From an unsigned review, *The North American Review*, Vol. 103, October 1866, pp. 557–63.

JOHN BLACKWOOD: 1866
A Publisher's Response to his Author's Manuscript

. . . The more I think over . . . these volumes of *Felix Holt* the more I am impressed . . . Mrs Transome and her maid are a perfect picture, and the description of the managing old lady's feelings when her son is so cool and taking the reins out of her hands and all her hopes are blasted is so painfully true. What a group are the old minister, Esther, and Felix in that dingy little house with Mrs Holt like a comic chorus in the background! . . . I am charmed with Esther and desperately anxious about her future. . . .

From a letter to George Eliot, 26 April 1866, *The George Eliot Letters*, Vol. 4, p. 244.

R. H. HUTTON: 1873
Middlemarch: a Study of Provincial Life

George Eliot has never displayed more imaginative and intellectual power than in this her latest and, in some important respects, her richest tale. There is more passion and more lofty conception in *Adam Bede*, more affluence of the provincial grotesques of English rural life in *The Mill on the Floss*, more beauty in *Silas Marner*, more curious intellectual subtlety in *Romola*; but none of them can really compare with *Middlemarch* for delicacy of detail and completeness of finish—

completeness as regards not only the individual figures, but the whole picture of rural society delineated—and for the breadth of life brought within the field of the story. It is, no doubt, as a mere story, inferior both to *Adam Bede* and to *Silas Marner*, the latter a perfect little gem of its kind, in which the author has done what is so rare with her—sacrificed something of her own deep feeling of the unsatisfactoriness of real life to the ideal demand for 'poetical justice', by rounding off the events somewhat more ideally than human lots are usually rounded off, in harmony with the author's and reader's inward sense of moral fitness, and scarcely in harmony with the average teaching of vigilant observation. And, yet, even in *Silas Marner*, she has left a certain spring of unhealed and undeserved pain to remind us of the deep unsatisfactoriness of human things; in the catastrophe of *Adam Bede*, we hardly know whether she has not left more rankling pain than satisfaction; and in *Romola*, the sense of foiled aims and wrecked purposes unquestionably predominates, so that we can hardly help thinking she was drawn to the subject of *Romola*, by perceiving a certain similarity between the spiritual illusions of the age of the great Dominican heretic and our own—a similarity which enables her to paint a great historical theme in her own favourite melancholy tone, without any violence to nature. And, now, in *Middlemarch*, George Eliot has set herself, from the very beginning, to illustrate her own profound conviction that the noblest aims, however, faithfully and simply pursued, are apt to be wrecked, at least to outward seeming, in this our modern age of distracted life. She sets herself to paint by no means a tragedy, but what she herself describes as 'a life of mistakes', the offspring of a 'certain spiritual grandeur, ill-matched with the meanness of opportunity'. And what she loses in beauty and in grandeur of effect by this deliberate aim, she seems to gain in ease, and in the obviously greater accordance between her array of intellectual and moral assumptions, and her artistic treatment of them. You feel that the inmost mind of the writer is reflected, not merely in the criticisms and the casual observations of the tale, but in the tale itself; you feel throughout the painful sincerity which underlies both the humour and the sarcasm; you feel the desolateness of the formative thought as well as the root of its bitterness, and yet you never cease to feel the author's extraordinary fidelity to her own moral aims. *Middlemarch* is, as the preface (unfortunately called a 'prelude') pretty plainly confesses, a sort of pictorial indictment of modern society for the crippling conditions it imposes on men and women, especially women, of high ideal enthusiasm. In consequence of the very aim of the tale, it could hardly be a satisfying imaginative whole, either tragic or otherwise; for the object is to paint not the grand defeat, but the helpless entanglement and miscarriage, of noble aims; to make us see the eager stream of high purpose, not leaping destructively from the rock, but more or less silted up, though not quite lost, in the dreary sands of modern life.

The very nature of this conception, while it ensures a certain vein of melancholy and even bitterness in the story, gives George Eliot's genius a fuller play than it has ever yet had for its predominant realism, and also for that minute knowledge of the whole moral field of modern life which alone tests the strength of a realistic genius. It was impossible to show how ideal aims could be frustrated and overborne by the mere *want of room* for them and the crowd of pettier thoughts and hopes in the society in which they were conceived, without a broad canvas and great variety of grouping; and this is exactly where George Eliot excels. To anyone who can endure the melancholy which is rather to be read between the lines than ostentatiously paraded, to anyone who either does not constantly ask himself how this great author is really conceiving the ultimate problems of faith and duty, or who, if understanding fully the nature of her answer, is steeled against the pain it is liable to give, the wonderful freshness and variety of the pictures of county society (high and low), the perfect drawing and bold outlines of her characters, and the minute delicacy of the lights and shades, the abundant humour, the caustic philosophy, and the deep undertone of unsatisfied desire, will give, if certainly not pure delight, all the pleasure which can be derived from profound and unaffected admiration. For artistic finish and breadth, *taken together*, George Eliot has no equal among novelists. Miss Austen rivalled, perhaps excelled, her in the former, and Sir Walter Scott surpassed her in the latter quality; but neither of them even approached her in the combination of the two. Certainly George Eliot cannot compare for a moment with Sir Walter Scott in historical portraiture. Savonarola is a mere shadow beside the splendid portraits of Mary Queen of Scots, or James I, or Louis XI, or Charles the Bold, all of which remind one of the full, rich painting of Titian's days. But with this great exception—of the art of re-animating the past—where, even in Scott, is such a store of faithful and finished pictures of character to be found? . . . George Eliot paints with Miss Austen's unerring humour and accuracy, and with Sir Walter's masculine breadth . . . She can draw not merely eccentric characters, but perfectly simple and normal characters of to-day, with all the humour and truth that Scott reserved for his special studies. She has Miss Austen's accuracy and instinct combined with a speculative sympathy with various grooves of thought which gives depth to the minutiae of real life, and which enables her to interest the intellect of her readers, as well as to engross their imagination. And these great powers have never been brought out with anything like the full success achieved in *Middlemarch*. As our author's object in this tale is to show the paralysis, and the mis-leading diversions from its natural course, which a blunt and unsym-pathetic world prepares for the noblest ideality of feeling that is not in sympathy with it, it was essential for her to give such a solidity and complexity to her picture of the world by which her hero's and heroine's idealism was to be more or less tested and partly subjugated, as would justify the impression that she understood fully the character of the struggle. We doubt if any other novelist who ever wrote could have

succeeded equally well in this melancholy design, could have framed
as complete a picture of English county and county-town society, with
all its rigidities, jealousies, and pettiness, with its thorough good-nature,
stereotyped habits of thought, and very limited accessibility to higher
ideas, and have threaded all these pictures together by a story, if not of
the deepest interest, still admirably fitted for its peculiar purpose of
showing how unplastic is such an age as ours to the glowing emotion of
an ideal purpose. . . .

For melancholy, profoundly melancholy, both in aim and execution,
Middlemarch certainly is; not that either hero or heroine dies within
its limits; on the contrary, the only deaths are deaths of people profoundly indifferent or disagreeable to the reader. And the heroine,
though she makes a sad blunder in her first marriage, marries the only
man she has ever loved at the end of the tale. Nay, there is another love
affair, which eventually prospers well, running through the tale; and
the only characters of any moment which are left in a certain cheerless
solitude at the close, are those of the young surgeon who has married the
woman of his choice, but found the choice a fatal mistake for himself,
and of the middle-aged and very Broad Church vicar, who shows to
much more advantage in giving up his love than he could have shown
in urging it, and who is made the occasion of giving us, perhaps, the only
really satisfying emotion which the story excites. The melancholy of
the story consists not in the catastrophes of fortune, but in the working
out of the only design with which the author set out—the picture 'of
the cygnet reared uneasily among the ducklings in the brown pond, and
who never finds the living stream in fellowship with its own oary-footed
kind'; in the delineation of what George Eliot (with a sentimentalism
and disposition to 'gush', of which she is hardly every guilty) calls the
'loving heart-beats and sobs after an unattained goodness', which
'tremble off' and are dispersed among hindrances instead of centring
in some long-recognisable 'deed.' The object of the book is gained by
showing in Dorothea's case that a rare nature of the most self-forgetting
kind, and the most enthusiastic love for the good and beautiful, is
rather more likely to blunder, in its way through the world, than one
of much lower moral calibre—which is probable enough; but also by
showing that this rare nature does not find any satisfying inward life
to compensate these blunders, and turn them into the conditions of
purer strength and less accidental happiness—which we should have
thought impossible; and again in Lydgate's case, by showing that an
ardent love for truth—of the purely intellectual kind—is liable to be
betrayed, by the commonplace good nature with which it is often
combined, into a paralysing contact with sordid cares and domestic
trials—which, again, is probable enough; but also by showing that his
love of truth is not transmuted into any higher moral equivalent through
the noble and genuine self-denial of the sacrifice made for another's
good—which, again, we should have held to be impossible. That Lydgate, marrying as he did, and with his wholesome nature, should before

long have merged the gratification of his disinterested, speculative passion in the necessity of considering the happiness of his shallow-natured wife, is most true to nature. That, in pursuing that course from the high and right motive from which, on the whole, he pursued it, he should have gained no new power over either her or himself, but should have become bitter on his side, and left her as vain and shallow as he found her, is, we trust, not true to nature, but a picture due to that set theory of melancholy realism which George Eliot evidently regards as the best substitute for faith. It is only here and there, in the rare glimpses she gives us of the solitude of Dorothea's heart, that this radical deficiency of faith is carried, as it seems to us, into any touch untrue to what we know of real life. It does so come out, we think, in one or two descriptions of Dorothea's secret struggles, and in the bitter tone in which the close of Lydgate's career is described. Generally, however, nothing can be more truthful or less like preconceived theory than the pictures of provincial life in this wonderful book. But not the less does this deep distrust of 'the Supreme Power', who, in the words of the 'prelude' to *Middlemarch*, has fashioned the natures of women 'with inconvenient indefiniteness', give a certain air of moral desolation to the whole book, and make us feel how objectless is that network of complicated motives and grotesque manners, of which she gives us so wonderfully truthful a picture—objectless as those strange scrawlings on the bare mountain side which, mistaken when seen from a distance for the handwriting of some gigantic power, turn out when approached to be the mere tracks of old destructive forces, since diverted into other channels—the furrows of dried-up torrents or the grooves of exhausted glaciers.

By far the most remarkable *effort* in *Middlemarch*—we are by no means sure that the success is quite in proportion to the effort, though the success is great, and one in which only a mind of great genius could have attained—is, of course, the sketch of Dorothea . . . it is the main idea of this book to work out the mal-adaptation, as it were, of this fresh, disinterested, and spiritual-minded girl, to the world into which she was born; to show that instead of giving her a full natural channel for her enthusiasm, and opening to her a career as large as her heart and mind, it, for a time at least, absorbed her great qualities in futile and fruitless efforts, which left hardly any one but herself the better for them; that it made her the victim of a sort of irony of destiny, gave her no chance of marriage with the one man—living in her neighbourhood and in circles where they frequently crossed each other's paths—whom she could perhaps have helped to something great and noble, and left her, even at the close, in no position better adapted to her rare qualities than that of the wife of a clever, mercurial, petulant young politician, not without good in him, but without any signal need of the help of such a woman as this, a woman who, as his wife, came to be 'only known in a certain circle as a wife and mother'. Yet no one who knows George Eliot will suppose that this history is meant to throw any doubt on the intrinsic value of high moral qualities. However negative our author's spiritual creed may be, her ethics are always noble. She makes us feel with ever-increasing force, as the story goes on, the intrinsic grandeur of Dorothea's capacity for self-forgetfulness, sympathy, and love. The story does not end without one signal triumph of the purity of her unselfish purpose over poorer and meaner natures, a triumph painted in a scene that deserves to rank for power beside that in which Dinah wins her victory over Hetty's guilty heart in *Adam Bede*. But while true as ever to her own passionate love of a deep and inward morality, our author is evidently anxious in these pages to show how ill-suited this world is to detect the highest natures that find their way into it, and to use them for the highest ends. Dorothea's desire to devote herself to someone wiser and deeper than herself, leads her into marrying the Rev. Edward Casaubon, a middle-aged, reserved, vain, and dry clergyman, given to laborious researches into a somewhat vague science, Comparative Mythology, for the full treatment of which he does not possess the adequate Oriental learning, nor even access to the German authorities who had made that learning their own. He acts upon Dorothea as a mere moral sponge, to absorb all the finer juices of her nature without being the happier or the better for them, rather, perhaps, the more irritable, and the worse. Her intellectual brightness, her power of perceiving that he himself distrusts his own power for his task, daunts him, and makes him feel under a sort of intellectual surveillance. Her ardent sympathy with his poor cousin, Mr. Ladislaw, and wish to befriend him, make Mr. Casaubon jealous, and dimly conscious of his own narrowness of nature. Her desire to share his deepest life makes him painfully conscious that he has no deepest life to be shared. Her ardour is a reproach to his formalism. Her enthusiasm is bewildering to his self-occupation. They lead together a life of mutual disappointment, in which her self-forgetful compassion for his broken health and his fear of intellectual wreck, gradually overpowers her own regrets, and she is on the very eve of promising him to carry out after his death, from his voluminous notes, his hopeless intellectual design—without the slightest remaining faith, on her part, in its value—when his sudden death relieves her of the necessity of making the fatal promise. Nothing can be finer than the picture of their mutual relations to each other; his reserved pride, her disappointed tenderness; his formal kindness and suspicious vigilance for his wife's distrust of his powers, her sickness of heart when she first begins to understand that his work will come to nothing, and to desire to give him a sympathy he cannot and will not receive. It is a picture such as no one but George Eliot could draw. . . . The rich spontaneous pity and sympathy of Dorothea are thrown into relief by that poverty of heart of Rosamond which is not even stirred by the most touching appeals of Lydgate's generous self-reproach. The deep, impulsive sincerity of Dorothea is thrown into like relief by that absolute absence of all compunction, of all discomposure, in insincerity, which Rosamond shows in hiding from her husband her counter-plots against his plans. Dorothea's perfect indifference to the world and rank is in striking contrast to poor Rosamond's positive pining after the society of titled people and the little excitements of social esteem. Dorothea's disposition to lavish herself and her means on others is in the most curious contrast of all to Rosamond's constant wish to get others to devote themselves to her. In short, it is impossible to conceive a finer foil to Dorothea than Rosamond. It is hard to say which lives to the fullest extent in the reader's mind; perhaps the realism of the portrait of Rosamond engrosses the imagination even more completely than the noble freshness and living ardour of Dorothea. But though to some extent they cross each other in the story, Rosamond wishing to detach Ladislaw from his love for Dorothea, they hardly meet, in any real contact of mind, till just at the close. And that meeting is a scene, we admit, of surpassing power. Dorothea, then a widow, assured, as she thinks, of Ladislaw's love for her, is bent on helping Lydgate, who, in the difficulties and false suspicions which have fallen on him, has just given her a glimpse of his wife's inability to understand his position; she has called on Rosamond, and found her own lover, Ladislaw, apparently bending in a lover-like attitude over Rosamond's hand, and has quitted the room, indignant, heart-broken. The night of anguish she passes after this scene is most powerfully described (though by the way with one false note: when did we ever before hear so true and refined a writer as George Eliot gushing about Dorothea's 'grand woman's frame', like a sentimental poetaster?); but the victory she gains over herself seems to us a victory that, in such a one as Dorothea at all events, could not have been gained without something more than a bare moral struggle. . . .

We must not dwell at the same length on the other parts of this wonderful photograph of provincial life; but it is well to point out the unity of thought which runs through it all, and also the artistic skill to combine with a full expression of love for the noble parts of human nature and an exquisite delineation of them, a pervading impression of 'the meanness of opportunity' that besets all noble aims, especially in provincial society in this century of ours. The most elaborate illustration of this, next to Dorothea's history, is Lydgate's. His earnest though purely intellectual thirst for scientific truth is far more completely defeated and subjugated by the meanness of opportunity than Dorothea's thirst for goodness, no doubt *because* it is purely intellectual, and because his moral nature, though manly and generous, has no particularly exalted aims. There are no scenes in English literature so full of power—the sort of power from the excess of which we almost shrink—as those in which Rosamond's thin, unyielding, inexpressible, and incompressible selfishness and worldliness of nature encounters and defeats the strong, masculine, magnanimous, generous struggles of Lydgate to overcome the difficulties caused by an improvident marriage, and to hold fast to his resolve of devoting his life to the higher scientific aims of physiological study, and not merely to winning his bread as a medical specialist. We cannot dwell on the picture, but we cannot leave it without saying that we think here, too, George Eliot has put too dark a ground into her canvas, and probably from the same cause as in the previous picture. . . .

The whole social picture both of town and county life in *Middlemarch*, though it is seldom cynical, and often most sympathetic in its portraiture of true nobility of character, is wonderfully vivid in its illustration of the pettiness and of the meanness of the aims generally pursued. Even Caleb Garth, the land surveyor, a noble figure, with his delight in honest work—which he praises in a phraseology of borrowed Scripture dialect from which the Scriptural ideas have disappeared—only shows his nobility by his benevolence, his integrity, his thoroughness, and his charity, but not by any vision of a life higher than that of the surveyor and land agent. Though he lives, within his small sphere, up to the full height of Christian purity and charity, his imagination dwells solely on his work of promoting benevolently the thorough cultivation of the land; capable as he is of great self-sacrifices to his own ideal of conduct, the author is anxious to make you see that Caleb Garth's ideal is of the purest secularistic type. Then Mr. Farebrother, a most winning character, is saved from his excusable but not very noble desire to win money at whist to add to his small savings, not by any effort of will, but by opportunity, which gives him a better living. It is true he triumphs manfully over the temptation his love for Mary Garth suggests to him, to let her younger and more favoured lover fall into bad ways without making an effort to save him; and here, for a second time in the story, 'the meanness of opportunity' is beaten by the spiritual fidelity of one of its characters. But these endeavours of noble character only bring out, and are intended to bring out, the poverty of the moral circumstances amidst which they move. Again, the whole account—and most powerful it is—of the illness and death of the old miser, Peter Featherstone, and of the conduct of his relatives—the brilliant if slightly overdrawn picture of the evangelical banker's fraud and crimes (when we call it overdrawn we refer to the complete absence of remorse in Mr. Bulstrode's demeanour on the day of the death of his victim. We do not believe that a man who had had such a conflict with his conscience on the previous night could have felt pure relief at the apparent success of his own guilt)—the account of Mr. Vincy's worldly selfishness—the jealousies of the medical men of Middlemarch —the ignorance and meanness of its shop-keepers—the moral vacuity of the country gentry, amongst whom leniency to the tenants and liberality as regards fencing and draining seem to be the highest moral aims of which they have any knowledge—and the clever but petty tittle-tattle of the country society—are all illustrations of the main idea of the book, that Dorothea's noble, ideal nature had been placed in a world not indeed of such evil, but of such mean opportunity, that it must have been badly straitened for want of congenial food and air. As poor Dorothea says in one place, 'I don't feel sure about doing good in any way now; *everything seems like going on a mission to people whose language I don't know*; unless it were building good cottages, there can be no doubt about that.' And the whole tale is founded on this mutual unintelligibility of Dorothea's language of the soul, and Middlemarch's language of the senses.

Indeed, it is the main function of the rich and abundant humour of *Middlemarch* to re-enforce the same idea. Richer and more abundant humour there has not been in any book of our own day; but delightful as it is, the general drift of it is to show up the petty moral scale of the society depicted. The most humorous picture in the book is probably that of Dorothea's uncle, Mr. Brooke, with his kindly penuriousness, his fragmentary literary interests, his intellectual shuffle, his dread of going far enough to mean anything, his scraps of reminiscence, and his mode of alleviating disagreeable news by introducing it 'among a number of disjointed particulars, as if it would get a milder flavour by mixing'. A more humorous picture than that of Mr. Brooke has hardly been produced in all the range of English literature; but it is obvious that its special significance in this story is to illustrate the ideal impotence of the society in which Dorothea was to figure, to give us a vivid impression of the intellectual and moral paralysis of the figures from whom chiefly Dorothea had to look for help and guidance. Then again, the extremely humorous picture of Mrs. Cadwallader, the aristocratic, witty, rector's wife, who is always cheapening, not only the commodities she buys, but the minds she encounters in the county society around her, is a perfect instrument for exhibiting the weaknesses and incoherences of the more important figures in *Middlemarch* in a pointed and striking form. . . .

That *Middlemarch* is a great and permanent addition to George Eliot's fame and to the rich resources of English literature we have no doubt. A book of more breadth of genius in conception, of more even execution, is hardly to be found in our language. No doubt it is a little tame in plot, but for that the depth of its purpose and the humour of its conversations sufficiently atone. The melancholy at the heart of it, no criticism of course can attenuate, for that is of its essence. George Eliot means to draw noble natures struggling hard against the currents of a poor kind of world, and without any trust in any invisible rock higher than themselves to which they can entreat to be lifted up. Such a picture is melancholy in its very conception. That in spite of this absence of any inward vista of spiritual hope, and in spite of the equally complete absence of any outward vista of 'far-resonant action', George Eliot should paint the noble characters in which her interest centres as clinging tenaciously to that *caput mortuum* into which Mr. Arnold has so strangely reduced the Christian idea of God—'a stream of tendency, not ourselves, which makes for righteousness',—and as never even inclined to cry out 'let us eat and drink, for to-morrow we die', is a great testimony to the ethical depth and purity of her mind. And it will add to the interest of *Middlemarch* in future generations, when at length this great wave of scepticism has swept by us, and 'this tyranny is overpast', that in pointing to it as registering the low-tide mark of spiritual belief among the literary class in the nineteenth century, the critics of the future will be compelled to infer from it, that even during that low ebb of trust in the supernatural element of religion, there was no want of ardent belief in the spiritual obligations of purity and self-sacrifice, nor even in that 'secret of the Cross' which, strangely enough, survives the loss of the faith from which it sprang.

From an unsigned review, *The British Quarterly Review*, Vol. 57. 1 April 1873, pp. 407–29 (407–12, 416–17, 420, 423–7, 429).

SAMUEL BUTLER: 1873
Middlemarch

... I call it bad ... The book seems to me to be a long-winded piece of studied brag, clever enough I dare say, but to me at any rate singularly unattractive. ...

From a letter to E. M. A. Savage, March 1873, in G. Keynes and Bt. Hill (eds) *Samuel Butler: Letters to E. M. A. Savage 1871–1885*. 1935, p. 40.

EMILY DICKINSON: 1873
The mysteries of human nature

'What do I think of *Middlemarch*?' What do I think of glory—except that in a few instances this 'mortal has already put on immortality.'

[1 *Corinthians* xv, 53] George Eliot is one. The mysteries of human nature surpass the 'mysteries of redemption', for the infinite we only suppose, while we see the finite ...

From a letter to Louise and Francis Norcross, late April 1873, in Thomas H. Johnson (ed.) *Letters of Emily Dickinson*, Vol. 2, The Belknap Press, Cambridge, Mass., 1958, p. 506.

LORD ACTON: 1881
A Historian's Tribute

... It is hard to say why I rate *Middlemarch* so high. There was a touch of failure in the two preceding books, in *Felix Holt*, and even in

Romola. And it was *Middlemarch* that revealed to me not only her grand serenity, but her superiority to some of the greatest writers. My life is spent in endless striving to make out the inner point of view, the *raison d'être,* the secret of fascination for powerful minds, of systems of religion and philosophy, and of politics, the offspring of the others, and one finds that the deepest historians know how to display their origin and their defects, but do not know how to think or to feel as men do who live in the grasp of the various systems. And if they sometimes do, it is from a sort of sympathy with the one or the other, which creates partiality and exclusiveness and antipathies. Poets are no better. Hugo, who tries so hard to do justice to the Bishop and the Conventionnel, to the nuns and the Jacobinical priest, fails from want of contact with the royalist nobleman and the revolutionary triumvirate, as Shakespeare fails ignobly with the Roman Plebs. George Eliot seems to me capable not only of reading the diverse hearts of men, but of creeping into their skin, watching the world through their eyes, feeling their latent background of conviction, discerning theory and habit, influences of thought and knowledge, of life and of descent, and having obtained this experience, recovering her independence, stripping off the borrowed shell, and exposing scientifically and indifferently the soul of a Vestal, a Crusader, an Anabaptist, an Inquisitor, a Dervish, a Nihilist, or a Cavalier without attraction, preference, or caricature. And each of them should say that she displayed him in his strength, that she gave rational form to motives he had imperfectly analysed, that she laid bare features in his character he had never realised. . . .

From a letter to Mary Gladstone, 21 January 1881, in H. Paul (ed.) *Letters of Lord Acton to Mary Gladstone,* 1913, pp. 46–47.

JOSEPH JACOBS: 1877
Mordecai: A Protest Against the Critics By a Jew

Sephardo

> Wise Books
> For half the truths they hold are honoured tombs.
>
> *Spanish Gypsy*

The critics have had their say: the recording angels of literature, more sorrowful than angry, have written down *Daniel Deronda* a failure. And there seems to be at least this much of truth in their judgement that one of the parts of which the book is composed has failed to interest or even to reach its audience. For the least observant reader must have noticed that *Daniel Deronda* is made up of two almost unconnected parts, either of which can be read without the other. Every 'book' after the first is divided into two parts, whose only claim to be included under the same covers is common action or inaction of the eponymous hero. One set of characters and interests centres round the fate and fortunes of Gwendolen Harleth, and of this part of the book we can surely say that it has excited as much interest and bitten as deeply into men's minds as any of the author's previous studies of female character. Indeed, we would submit that George Eliot's last portrait of female egoism is in many ways her best; her hand has become more tender, and, because more tender, more true than when she drew such narrow types as Hetty Sorrel and Rosamond Vincy, so unnaturally consistent in their selfishness. The story of Gwendolen Harleth's purification from egoism is then, one might say, even a greater success than the former pictures of girlish struggles, and displays the author's distinguishing excellences in undiminished brilliancy. But there is another part of the book with which the English-speaking public and its literary 'tasters' have failed to sympathise, and which they have mostly been tempted to omit on reperusal. The tragedy of Mordecai Cohen's missionary labours, on which the author has spent immense labour of invention and research, must be pronounced to have completely failed in reaching and exciting the interest and sympathy of the ordinary reader. Mr. Bagehot has told us that the greatest pain man can feel is the pain of a new idea, and the readers of *Daniel Deronda* have refused painfully to assimilate the new idea of the Mordecai part of the book. This idea we take to be that Judaism stands on the same level as Christianity, perhaps even on a higher level, in point of rationality and capacity to satisfy the wants of the religious consciousness, 'the hitherto neglected reality', to use the author's own words . . . 'that Judaism is something still throbbing in human lives, still making for them the only conceivable vesture of the world.' The difficulty of accepting this new idea comes out most prominently in the jar most readers must have felt in the omission of any explanation of the easy transition of Deronda from the Christianity in which he was bred to the Judaism in which he had been born.

The present notice proposes to discuss the failure of this unsuccessful part, from the standpoint of one for whom this initial difficulty does not exist, and who has from his childhood seen the world habited in those Hebrew Old Clothes of which Mr. Carlyle and others have spoken so slightingly. And the first thing that it is natural for a Jew to say about *Daniel Deronda* is some expression of gratitude for the wonderful completeness and accuracy with which George Eliot has portrayed the Jewish nature. Hitherto the Jew in English fiction has fared unhappily: being always represented as a monstrosity, most frequently on the side of malevolence and greed, as in Marlowe's Barabbas and Dickens's Fagin, or sometimes, as in Dicken's Riah, still more exasperatingly on the side of impossible benevolence. What we want is truth, not exaggeration, and truth George Eliot has given us with the large justice of the great artist. The gallery of Jewish portraits contained in *Daniel Deronda* gives in a marvellously full and accurate way all the many sides of our complex national character. The artistic element, with the proper omission of painting and sculpture, in which Jews, though eminent, have not been pre-eminent, is well represented by Klesmer, Mirah and the Alcharisi. Ezra Cohen is a type of the commonplace Jew, the familiar figure of prosperous mercantile dealing, the best known trait of Jews to Englishmen; while little Jacob exhibits in a very humorous form the well-known precocity of Jewish children. The affectionate relations of Ezra Cohen and his mother and the tender respect of Mordecai and Mirah for the memory of theirs, point to the exceptional influence of the Mother and the Home in the inner life of Jews. Then in Kalonyneos, whom we feel tempted to call the Wandering Jew, we get the nomadic spirit which has worked in Israel from times long previous to the Dispersion, while all must join in the scorn the author evidently feels for Pash, the Jew who is no Jew. Yet he is the representative of what might be called the Heine side of Jewry—the wit and cynicism that reached their greatest intensity in the poet of Young Germany. The more temperate Gideon represents, it is to be feared, a large proportion of English Jews, one not ashamed of his race, yet not proud of it, and willing to see the racial and religious distinctions we have fought for so valiantly die out and perish utterly among men. Perhaps the most successful of the minor portraits is that of the black sheep Lapidoth, the Jew with no redeeming love for family, race, or country to preserve him from that sordid egoism (the new name for wickedness) into which he has sunk. His utter unconsciousness of good and evil is powerfully depicted in the masterly analysis of his state of mind before purloining Deronda's ring. To some extent the weird figure of the Alcharisi serves as a sort of companion-picture of female renunciation of racial claims but the struggle between her rebellious will and what old-fashioned folk call the Will of God (Professor Clifford would perhaps name it the Tribal Will) raises her to a tragic height which makes Deronda's mother perhaps the most imposing figure in the book. Deronda himself, by the circumstance of his education, is prevented from typifying any of the social distinctions of a Jew, yet it is not unlikely that his gravity of manner and many-sided sympathy were meant by the author to be taken as hereditary traits.

These, with Ram the bookseller, the English Jew of the pre-emancipation era, and some minor characters, give to the reader a most complete picture of Jews and Jewesses in their habits as they live, of Jews and Jewesses as members of a peculiar people in relation to the Gentile world. To point the moral of human fallibility, besides some minor slips in ceremonial details on which it were ungrateful to dwell, [Taliths or fringed mantles are not worn on Friday nights, the Kaddish, or prayer, in honour of the dead, is only said for eleven months, not eleven years, and then only by a son. Mirah seems to be under the same delusion. Before breaking the bread Cohen should have 'made Kiddush', *i.e.* pronounced a blessing over some sacramental wine. It is doubtful whether Cohen would have paid money and written a pawn-ticket on

Sabbath eve, but this may be intentional][1] we cannot but think (a critic is nothing if not critical) that the author has failed to give in Mirah an adequate type of Jewish girlhood. Mirah is undoubtedly tame; and tameness, for those who know them, is the last infirmity of Jewish girls. Still even here the sad experience of Mirah's youth may be held to have somewhat palliated any want of brightness, and the extra vivacity of Mrs. Cohen junior perhaps supplies the deficiency.

So much for the outer life of Judaism. The English reader will find here no idea so startlingly novel, as to raise opposition to its admission, or to disturb his complacent feeling of superiority over Jews in all but a certain practical sagacity (he calls it sharpness or cunning), which must be postulated to explain the 'differentia of success' characterising the Jewish species of commercial dealings. One new fact he may indeed profitably learn; from the large group of Jewish characters in *Daniel Deronda* he may perhaps gather that there are not all Lapidoths, nor even all Ezra Cohens, as he has been accustomed to think.

But the new idea of which we have spoken is embodied in the person of Mordecai Cohen, the Jew *par excellence* of the book, the embodiment of the inner life of Judaism. The very fact of this recognition of an inner life, not to speak of the grand personality in which she has typified it, entitles George Eliot to the heart-deep gratitude of all Jews; the more so inasmuch as she has hazarded and at least temporarily lost success for her most elaborated production by endeavouring to battle with the commonplace and conventional ideas about Judaism. The present article aims at striking another blow to convince the English world of the existence in the present day and for all past time of a spiritual life in Judaism. And we can conceive of no better point of defence for the position than the historic probability of the character of Mordecai, which critics have found so mystic, vague, and impossible.

Those who know anything of the great leaders of spiritual Judaism will recognise in Mordecai all the traits that have characterized them. Saul of Tarsus, Ibn Gebirol (Avicebron), Jehuda Halevi, Ibn Ezra, Maimonides, Spinoza, Mendelssohn, not to mention other still more unfamiliar names, were all men like Mordecai: rich in inward wealth, yet content to earn a scanty livelihood by some handicraft; ardently spiritual, yet keenly alive to the claims of home affection; widely erudite, yet profoundly acquainted with human nature; mystics, yet with much method in their mysticism. The author seems even to have a bolder application of the historic continuity of the Hebraic spirit in view: she evidently wishes Mordecai to be regarded as a 'survival' of the prophetic spirit, a kind of Isaiah redivivus. Hence a somewhat unreal effect is produced by his use of a diction similar to what might be expected from a 'greater Prophet' stepping out of the pages of the Authorised Version. Still it is to be remembered that we almost always

---

[1] Square brackets indicate footnotes incorporated into the text.

see Mordecai in states of intense excitement, when his thought would naturally clothe itself in the forms in which all his literary efforts had been written. He speaks in a sufficiently prosaic, and unbiblical style when the subject is prosaic, as to Daniel Deronda at their first meeting. . . . : 'What are you disposed to give for it?' 'I believe Mr. Ram will be satisfied with half-a-crown, sir,' remarks sufficiently on the level of nineteenth-century conversation to give Mordecai some community with ordinary folk.

There is yet another quality which Mordecai shares with the sages and prophets of the past: he is a layman . . . Mordecai shares yet another gift of his predecessors: he is a poet. The fragment in chapter XXXVIII, commencing—'Away from me the garment of forgetfulness, Withering the heart', might well be a translation from a Piut of Ibn Gebirol or a Selicha of Jehuda Halevi, and makes him a fit *dramatis persona* of that 'national tragedy in which the actors have been also the heroes and the poets'. . . . To believers in the principle of Heredity this would be enough to give to Mordecai that possibility which is sufficient for artistic existence. English critics, however, seem not to believe in hereditary influences: they have unanimously pronounced him an impossibility. They require, it would appear, some more tangible proof of the existence among modern Jews of a character like Mordecai's than the *a priori* probability afforded by the consideration of the historic continuity of national character. Even this want could be supplied . . . Surely the critics had no occasion to doubt the possibility of a Jew like Mordecai at a time when we are still mourning the loss of one who laid down his life for the regeneration of our views of Israel's past as Mordecai sacrificed his for the elevation of our hopes of Israel's future. 'I have certain words in my possession', wrote Emanuel Deutsch,[2] 'which have been given me that they might be said to others, few of many. . . . I know also that I shall not find peace or rest until I have said my whole say. And yet I cannot do it. And I yearn for things which I see and which might have been mine and would have been blessing and sunshine and the cooling dew to the small germs within me—and yet! and yet!—'

Would that Mr. Deutsch had lived to convince the world in his own burning words that Mordecai is no inert scarecrow of abstractions, but a warm living reality!

We have laid so much stress upon the artistic truth of Mordecai's character because, if this be granted, it is inexplicable that the central incident of the Jewish part of *Daniel Deronda*, the meeting on the bridge between him and Deronda, should have failed to strike readers as perhaps the most remarkable incident in English fiction. If Mordecai has artistic reality we contend that the meeting on the bridge in chapter XL reaches a tragic intensity which almost transcends the power of the novel, and would perhaps require the manifold emotive inlets of the Wagnerian drama to do it justice: eye, ear, brain and heart should all

[2] *The Literary Remains of the late Emanuel Deutsch*, 1874, p. xii.

be responsible. We boldly deny greater tragic intensity to any incident in Shakespeare. Nor are there wanting signs that the author herself, no contemptible critic of her own productions, sets an equal value on the incident. In the motto prefixed to chapter XXXVIII, describing Mordecai's yearnings, she tells us in Brownesque English—

'There be who hold that the deeper tragedy were a Prometheus bound, not *after*, but *before*, he had well got the celestial fire into the γάρθηξ, whereby it might be conveyed to mortals. Thrust by the Kratos and Bia of instituted methods into a solitude of despised ideas, fastened in throbbing helplessness by the fatal pressure of poverty and disease—a solitude where many pass by, but none regard.'

In other words, George Eliot considers the circumstances of Mordecai's fate to surpass in tragic pathos the most colossal monument of Greek dramatic art. Notice, too, the care with which she leads up to the incident. In the chapter XXXVII we have Deronda coming to the Meyricks at Chelsea to announce to Mirah the forthcoming visit of Klesmer, and the chapter finishes as he is leaving Chelsea. The next chapter . . . is filled with a description of Mordecai's yearning for a spiritual successor, and gives us *en passant* a fine picture of the scene of the meeting. . . . We get here in short all we need to understand and sympathise with the final episode of the 'book'; but lest we should come upon the fulfilment of the prophecy with too vivid a memory of the author's sublimation of the idea of prophecy, we have interposed, like a comic scene in an Elizabethan tragedy, the magnificent account of Klesmer's visit to the Meyricks in chapter XXXIX, which clearly occurred *after* the events described in chapter XL, which takes up the stream of narrative from chapter XXXVII.

It seems to us clear that all this seemingly inartistic transposition of events is intended to make the incident of chapter XL stand out more sharply into relief. We have the miracle explained away, it is true—the modern analytic spirit requires it—but the author wishes us to forget the explanation, or at least to relegate the intellectual element of chapter XXXVIII to the unconscious background, where it may be ready to assist, though not present to obstruct, emotion. All this care appears to show the importance attached by the author to the last chapter of book v.

And in itself, apart from what the author may think of it, what a soul-moving incident is there contained! A representative of an ancient world-important people, whose royalty of wrongs makes the aristocracies of Europe appear petty, finds himself clutched by the gripping hands of want and death before he can move the world to that vision of the Phoenix-rise of Israel which the prophetic instincts of his race have brought up clear before him. Careless of his own comfort, careless of coming death, he desires only to live anew—as the quasi-Positivist doctrine of the Cabala bids him live—in 'minds made nobler by his presence'. His prophetic vision pictures to him the very lineaments of his spiritual *alter ego*, whom he pathetically thinks of as differing from himself in all externals, and, as death draws nigh, the very scene of their meeting. And in this nineteenth century, in prosaic London, this inward vision of the poor consumptive Jew is fulfilled to the letter.

Would it be too bold a suggestion if we suspected the author of having typified in the meeting of Deronda and Mordecai that 'One far-off divine event, To which the whole creation moves', the meeting of Israel and its Redeemer? In personal characteristics, in majestic gravity (we cannot imagine Deronda laughing), in width of sympathy and depth of tenderness, even in outward appearance, Daniel resembles the great Galilean Pharisee whom all Christendom has accepted as in very truth the Messiah that will restore Judaea to the Holy People. To say the least, the author suggests the audacity in her comparison of the two to the figures of Jesus and the Pharisee in Titian's 'Tribute Money'.

We do not remember a single criticism . . . which has referred to this magnificent scene, where to our mind George Eliot's power of representing soul speaking to soul has reached its greatest height. We do not remember a single critic who seemed to think that Mordecai's fate was in any way more pitiful than that of any other consumptive workman with mystic and impossible ideas. What reasons can be given for this defect of sympathy? In addition to the before-mentioned assumption that Mordecai does not possess artistic reality, there has been the emotional obstruction to sympathy with a Jew, and the intellectual element of want of knowledge about modern Judaism. If Mordecai had been an English workman laying down his life for the foundation of some English International with Deronda for its Messiah Lassalle, he would have received more attention from the critics. But a Jew with views involving issues changing the future history of Humanity—'impossible, vague, mystic'. Let us not be misunderstood: the past generation of englishmen has been so generous to Jews that we should be ungrateful if we accused cultured Englishman of the present day of being *consciously* repelled by the idea of a poor Jew being worthy of admiration. But fifteen centuries of hatred are not to be wiped out by any legislative enactment. No one can say that the fact of a man's being a Jew makes no more difference in other men's minds than if he were (say) a Wesleyan. There yet remains a deep unconscious undercurrent of prejudice against the Jew which conscientious Englishmen have often to fight against as part of that lower nature, a survival of the less perfect development of our ancestors, which impedes the Ascent of Man.

Along with this unconscious Judaeophobia there has gone the intellectual element of a tacit assumption that modern Judaism is a lifeless code of ritual instead of a living body of religious truth. Of course the pathos and tragedy of Mordecai's fate depend in large measure on the value of the ideas for which he laid down his life. If he were a crazy believer that the English nation is descended from the lost Ten Tribes, his fate would only deserve a smile of contemptuous pity. Hence the artistic necessity of the philosophic discussion in chapter XLII, where his ideas are explained and defended. Here again we have to complain of the want of sympathy shown by the critics, but perhaps still more of their want of knowledge. Our author devotes the forty-first chapter to a piece of special pleading (really addressed to the reader, though supposed to be a philosophic musing of Deronda's), the outcome of which is that if we want to tell whether an enthusiast is justified in his faith, our only test is knowledge of the subject-matter. And the moral naturally is: study the history of the Jews. Hegel says somewhere—"The heritage a great man leaves the world is to force it to explain him, and we may say the same of a great work of art. But the critics of *Daniel Deronda* have refused to pay the heavy probate duty of wading through the ten volumes or so of Gratz's *Geschichte der Juden* to see whether Mordecai's ideas have anything in them or no: the easier plan was to denounce them as 'vague and mystical'. If it be contended that the subject is too unfamiliar for ordinary readers, and therefore unsuited for a novel, we may answer that similar reasoning would exalt an Offenbach over a Beethoven. George Eliot had endeavoured to raise the novel to heights where it may treat of subjects hitherto reserved for the Drama or the Epic, but instead of encouragement from English critics she meets with their neglect.

Apart, however, from the intrinsic value of Mordecai's ideas, the discussion would deserve our admiration as a literary *tour de force*. It was the high praise of the Greek philosopher that if the gods spoke Greek they would talk as Plato wrote: may we not say that if Isaiah had spoken English he would have prophesied as George Eliot makes Mordecai speak? We trace in this the influence which the Authorised Version,—with all its inaccuracies, the most living reproduction of the Hebrew Scriptures—has had on our principal writers, notably in the case of so unbiblical a writer as Mr. Swinburne.

And what of the ideas which Mordecai clothes with words as of one whose lips have been touched with coals of burning fire? What vagueness or mystery is there in the grand and simple lines of Jewish policy laid down by Mordecai? Two ideas dominate Mordecai's arguments throughout the discussion. The resumption of the soil of Palestine by the Jews (which has often been proposed by Gentile writers as a solution of the much vexed Eastern Question), and as a consequence the third and final promulgation of the Jewish religion to the world, are sufficiently definite ideas, however large and grand they may be. Even if one disagrees with Mordecai's views one may at any rate pay him the respect due to an energetic leader of the opposition, and recognise in him the leader of those who refuse to believe that Israel's part in history is played out, and that her future policy should be to amalgamate with the nations as soon as possible, letting her glorious past sink into an antiquarian study instead of living as a perennial spring of political action. Mordecai is not of those who hold that the millennium will come when men shall have arrived at that nicely balanced mediocrity, that the 'pale abstract' man shall know his brother from other cosmopolitan beings only by some official badge necessary for distinction. He rather holds that in the world-organism of the nations each nationality will have its special function, Israel, as the Jewish poet-philosopher said, being the nations' hearts. [*Cusari*, ii, 36. Mordecai attributes the saying to Jehuda Halevi; Sephardo in the *Spanish Gypsy*, . . . to the *Book of Light*, the Cabalistic book Sohar. It occurs in both. . . .] The now-prevailing doctrine of Heredity and the political enthusiasm for Pan-slavism, Panteutonism, Pan-whatnotism, will have nought to urge against these Panjudaic views. And to our minds Mordecai's is the profounder philosophy of history when he further thinks that the great quarry of religious truth, whence two world-religions have been hewn and shaped, but only into torsos, has yet where-withal to completely fashion the religion of the future. . . .

What we have attempted to show has been that the adverse criticism on the Mordecai part of *Daniel Deronda* has been due to lack of sympathy and want of knowledge on the part of the critics, and hence its failure is not (if we must use the word) objective. If a young lady refuses to see any pathos in Othello's fate because she dislikes dark complexions, we blame the young lady, not Shakespeare; and if the critics have refused to see the pathos of Mordecai's fate because he is a Jew of the present day—so much the worse for the critics!

We have not attempted to criticise *Daniel Deronda* as a whole. Whether it errs in the juxtapositions of two parts appealing to such widely diverse interests, or in the position of the hero—which seems to partake of that unstable equilibrium which the proverb assigns to him that sitteth on two stools—or in the frequent introduction of physio-logical psychology couched in Spenserian phraseology, we have not cared to inquire. We have only spoken because we have some of the knowledge and all of the sympathy which alone, we contend, are needed to make the Mordecai part of *Daniel Deronda* as great a success as all must acknowledge to have attended the part relating to Gwendolen Harleth. If this be so, the lovers of English literature will have the gratification of knowing that the hand of one of our greatest artists has not lost its cunning, in these last days. Indeed, if a higher subject argue higher faculties, the successful treatment of a great world-problem would seem to be an advance on her previous studies of village life. . . .

From a signed review, *Macmillan's Magazine*, Vol. 36, June 1877, pp. 101–11 (101–08, 111).

ANTHONY TROLLOPE: 1874; 1876
Two Views of George Eliot

. . . I do not quite agree in all your criticism, touching A. Thackeray & G. Elliot;—not that I do not like Annie's work, but that I prefer

George Elliot's. . . . She is sometimes heavy—sometimes abstruse, sometimes almost dull, but always like an egg, full of meat. . . .

From a letter to Mary Holmes, 18 September 1874.

. . . Daniel D. has been a trying book to me. You know how I love and admire her. . . . But I think D. D. is all wrong in art. Not only is the oil flavoured on every page, (which is a great fault)—but with the smell of the oil comes so little of the brilliance which the oil should give! She is always striving for effects which she does not produce. All you say of Gwendoline's character is true. She disgusts, and does not interest, as a woman may even though she disgusts. . . .

From a letter to Mary Holmes, 27 May 1876. Both in B. A. Booth (ed.) *Letters of Anthony Trollope*, 1951, pp. 323, 354.

GEORGE HENRY LEWES: 1877
'We Only See What interests Us'

. . . We only see what interests us, and we have only insight in proportion to our sympathy. Now both these fundamental principles are forgotten by critics who ask, 'Who can be expected to feel interest in the Jews?'—'Who can believe in such a prig as Deronda?'—'Mordecai is a Shadow,' etc. . . .

From a letter to Edward Dowden, [February?] 1877, quoted in *The George Eliot Letters*, Vol. 6, pp. 336–7. The views Lewes characterized are to be found in the frequently reprinted, Henry James, 'Daniel Deronda: A Conversation' *The Atlantic Monthly*, Vol. 38, December 1876, pp. 684–94.

ROBERT L. STEVENSON: 1877
'A Rather Dry Lady'

. . . George Eliot: a high, but, may we not add?—a rather dry lady. Did you have a kick at the stern works of that melancholy puppy and humbug Daniel Deronda himself?—the Prince of Prigs; the literary abomination of desolation in the way of manhood; a type which is enough to make a man foreswear the love of women, if that is how it must be gained. . . . Hats off all the same you understand: a woman of genius. . . .

From a letter to A. Pritchett Martin, December 1877, in S. Colvin (ed.) *Letters of Robert Louis Stevenson*, 1902, Vol. I, p. 123.

SIGMUND FREUD: 1882
'Intimate Ways'

. . . Freud mentions . . . *Middlemarch*; this appealed to him very much
and he found it illuminated aspects of his relations with Martha
[Martha Bernays whom Freud married after a prolonged separation] . . .
Daniel Deronda amazed him by its knowledge of Jewish intimate ways
that 'we speak of only among ourselves'.

From Ernest Jones, *Sigmund Freud: Life and Work*, 1953–7, Vol. I,
p. 191. Jones is quoting from a letter of Freud's to Martha Bernays,
26 August 1882.

LESLIE STEPHEN: 1902
Felix Holt, George Eliot's Poetry,
Middlemarch, Daniel Deronda

. . . If we are to accept the indication given by the title, and suppose that
Felix Holt is to be the focus of interest, the novel, I think, fails of its
effect. We no more see the rough, thorough-going radicals, stung to
fury by pauperism and the slavery of children in factories, and sharing
the zeal and the illusions of Jacobins, than we saw the true spirit of the
Renaissance in *Romola*. Mr. Felix Holt would have been quite in his
place at Toynbee Hall; but is much too cold-blooded for the time when
revolution and confiscation were really in the air. Perhaps this
indicates the want of masculine fibre in George Eliot and the deficient
sympathy with rough popular passions which makes us feel that he
represents the afterthought of the judicious sociologist and not the man
of flesh and blood who was the product of the actual conditions. Anyhow, the novel appears to be regarded as her least interesting. There are
undoubtedly many charming scenes. One would be disposed to think
that Rufus Lyon, the old dissenting minister, was more of a contemporary of Baxter than could have been possible at the time; but one
cannot say confidently what survivals of the type there may have been
at Coventry, and his simplicity and pedantry and power of emphasising
the highest elements in the creed of his sect show the art of a skilled
humorist. Esther, too, with her naïve appreciation of the charms of a
luxurious life, is too good for Felix. But the really strongest part of
the novel is old Mrs. Transome, brooding over her sorrows, and
dwelling remorsefully upon her error in the past. "If she had only been
more haggard and less majestic, those who had glimpses of her outward
life might have said that she was a griping harridan with a tongue like a
razor. No one said exactly that; but they never said anything like the
full truth about her, or divined what was hidden under her outward
life—a woman's keen sensibility and dread, which lay screened behind
all her petty habits and narrow notions as some quivering thing with

eyes and throbbing heart may lie crouching behind withered rubbish. The sensibility and dread had paplitated all the faster in the prospect of her son's return; and now that she had seen him, she said to herself in her bitter way, 'It is a lucky cub that escapes skinning. The best happiness I shall ever know will be to escape the worst misery'." That is one of the striking passages in which George Eliot shows her vivid insight into certain moods and characters, Mrs. Transome, I confess, interests me so much that I should have liked to know a little more about that early intrigue which has soured her, and how she came to be fascinated by the old lover, who by the time at which the book opens has shown his inferior nature and uses the old memories to insult her. I could willingly have spared, in order to make room for a little more of the family scandal, some of the elaborate legal complications, and of Mr. Felix Holt's clumsy performances as a prophet of social reform. . . .

Paradise Lost is a masterpiece poetically, though its theology is grotesque and its proposed justification of Providence an admitted failure. Can we say anything of the kind on behalf of the *Spanish Gypsy*? It may clearly be said that it certainly shows a powerful intellect stored with noble sentiment and impelled to utter great thoughts. It illustrates curiously the union observed by Lewes of great diffidence with great ambition. She aims at the highest mark, though at any given moment she is despondent of achievement. She adopted the title of the poem, she says, because it recalled the old dramatists, with whom she thought she had 'more cousinship than with recent poets'.[3] It seems to have been first written in the dramatic form; though, as finished, it became a set of scenes interspersed with digressions into epic poetry. The passages which would be represented in the regular drama by stage directions are expanded into descriptive writing or into psychological disquisitions intended to introduce us to the characters. The old dramatists, to whom she refers, might give a precedent for introducing a good many sententious remarks upon human life which have no very direct relation to the story; but, in truth, she reminds us rather of 'Phillip van Artevelde', and other modern plays not intended for the stage; and if we complain that the book tried by dramatic tests becomes languid, it may be replied that we have had fair notice that it belongs to a different genus and should be judged from the author's point of view. This, however, does not answer the ordinary objection that, after all, it is not poetry; or does not decisively cross the indefinable but essential line which divides true poetry from the highest rhetoric. Here and there is a fine phrase, as in the opening passage about—

> Broad-breasted Spain, leaning with equal love
> On the Mid Sea that moans with memories,
> And on the untravelled Ocean's restless tides.

Or a few lines later—

[3] Middleton's *Spanish Gipsie* was acted about 1621.

What times are little? To the sentinel
That hour is regal when he mounts on guard.

Passages often sound exactly like poetry; and yet, even her admirers
admit that they seldom, if ever, have the genuine ring. They do not
satisfy the old criterion that nothing can be poetry, in the full sense, of
which we are disposed to say that it would be as good in prose. The
lyrics which are interspersed are palpable if clever imitations of the
genuine thing. Perhaps it was simply that George Eliot had not one
essential gift—the exquisite sense for the value of words which may
transmute even common thought into poetry. Even her prose, indeed,
though often admirable, sometimes becomes heavy, and gives the impression that instead of finding the right word she is accumulating more
or less complicated approximations. Then one might inquire whether,
after all, the problem of 'incarnating' the abstract idea, if not really
impracticable from the beginning, was suited to her powers. The dramatic form especially demands the intuitive instead of the discursive
attitude of mind, and the vivid 'presentation' of concrete men and
women instead of the thoughtful analysis of their character. Might she
not succeed by accepting the conditions frankly, and attempting, in
spite of its bad name, an avowedly 'philosophical form?' She loved
Wordsworth well enough to forgive his admitted shortcomings; and if
the *Excursion* is undeniably dull, it is still a work which, in spite of all
critical condemnations, has profoundly impressed the spiritual development of many eminent persons.

George Eliot was in fact led to try various poetical experiments. A
volume of poems published in 1874 contained the 'Legend of Jubal',
begun in 1869, 'How Lisa loved the King' (from Boccaccio), 'Agatha',
'Armgart', and 'A College Breakfast Party', which were written in the
same period. That they all show great literary ability is undeniable,
though it is still doubtful whether they show more. The 'College
Breakfast', with its downright plunge into metaphysics, set forth with
an abundant display of metaphor and illustration, is a singular exhibi-
tion of (as I must think) misapplied ingenuity; and chiefly interesting to
people who may wish to know George Eliot's judgement of Hegelianism,
aetheticism, and positivism. The most remarkable, however, is the short
poem called 'O may I join the choir invisible'. It has been accepted by
many who sympathise with her religious views. The invisible choir is
formed of those 'immortal dead who live again in minds made better
by their presence'. So to live, we are told, 'is heaven'. The generous
natures have set their example before us, and our 'rarer, better, truer
self' finds in them a help to harmonise discordant impulses, and seek a
loftier ideal.

The better self shall live till human Time
Shall fold its eyelids, and the human sky
Be gathered like a scroll within the tomb

Unread for ever.
This is life to come
Which martyred men have made more glorious
For us who strive to follow. May I reach
That purest heaven, be to other souls
The cup of strength in some great agony,
Enkindle generous ardour, feed pure love,
Beget the smiles that have no cruelty—
Be the sweet presence of a good diffused,
And in diffusion ever more intense.
So shall I join the choir invisible
Whose music is the gladness of the world.

To appreciate the sacred poetry of any church, one ought to be an orthodox member; and, to many people, of course, immortality thus understood, seems to be rather a mockery. It would be better, they think, to admit frankly that immortality is a figment. Even they may agree that the aspiration is lofty and eloquently expressed. Reflections upon a similar theme inspire two other poems. Armgart is a *prima donna*, rejoicing in the overpowering success of her first appearance, who suddenly loses her voice by a sudden attack of throat disease; and has to reconcile herself to the abandonment of her hopes, and to becoming part of the choir inaudible. 'Jubal'—which seems to me to be the nearest approach to genuine poetry—is the story of the patriarch who invented music. He leaves his tribe for a journey which, as he has the prediluvian longevity, is protracted for an indefinite time, and when he returns finds that people have got out of the habit of living for centuries. The descendents of his contemporaries are celebrating a feast in honour of the inventor of music; and, when he innocently observes that he is the person in question, he is pooh-poohed without further inquiry. As he lies down to die his Past appears to him, and explains that he should be content with having bestowed the great gift upon mankind. . . . The excellent R. H. Hutton was offended by the doctrine of this poem, especially by the apparent implication that death is, on the whole, a good thing, because it induced a race, which had taken things too easily as long as they fancied that they had an indefinite time before them, to rouse themselves and invent musical as well as other instruments. The logic indeed—if really intended—does not appear to be very cogent. The moral that, as we have got to die, we should be content with the consciousness of having played our part, without expecting reward or bothering ourselves about posthumous fame, is more to the purpose. Jubal, who happily lived in a purely legendary region, does not come into conflict with historical facts like Fedalma, and may be taken as a satisfactory poetical symbol of a characteristic mood, suggested by the old thought of mortality and oblivion. I cannot, indeed, believe that George Eliot achieved a permanent position in English poetry: she is a remarkable, I suppose unique, case, of a writer taking to poetry at the ripe age of forty-four, by which the majority of poets have done their best work. Perhaps that suggests that the impulse was acquired rather than innate, and more likely to seucced in impressing reflective and melancholy minds than in vivid presentation of concrete images. . . .

This, I think, explains the rather painful impression which is made by *Middlemarch*. It is prompted by a sympathy for the enthusiast, but turns out to be virtually a satire upon the modern world. The lofty nature is to be exhibited struggling against the circumambient element of crass stupidity and stolid selfishness. But that element comes to represent the dominant and overpowering force. Belief is in so chaotic a state that the idealist is likely to go astray after false lights. Intellectual ambition mistakes pedantry for true learning; religious aspiration tempts acquiescence in cant and superstition; the desire to carry your creed into practice makes compromise necessary, and compromise passes imperceptibility into surrender. One is tempted to ask whether this does not exaggerate one aspect of the human tragicomedy. The unity, to return to our 'parable', is to be the light carried by the observer in search of an idealist. In *Middlemarch* the light shows the aspirations of the serious actors and measures their excellence by their capacity for such a motive. The test so suggested seems to give a rather one-sided view of the world. The perfect novelist, if such a being existed, looking upon human nature from a thoroughly impartial and scientific point of view would agree that such aspirations are rare and obviously impossible for the great mass of mankind. People, indisputably, are 'mostly fools' and care very little for theories of life and conduct. But, therefore, it is, idle to quarrel with the inevitable or to be disappointed at its results; and, moreover, it is easy to attach too much importance to this particular impulse. The world, somehow or other, worries along by means of very commonplace affections and very limited outlooks. George Eliot, no doubt, fully recognises that fact, but she seems to be dispirited by the contemplation. The result, however, is that she seems to be a little out of touch with the actual world, and to speak from a position of philosophical detachment which somehow exhibits her characters in a rather distorting light. For that reason *Middlemarch* seems to fall short of the great masterpieces which imply a closer contact with the world of realities and less preoccupation with certain speculative doctrines. Yet it is clearly a work of extraordinary power, full of subtle and accurate observation; and gives, if a melancholy, yet an undeniably truthful portraiture of the impression made by the society of the time upon one of the keenest observers, though upon an observer looking at the world from a certain distance, and rather too much impressed by the importance of philosophers and theorists. . . .

The story of Gwendolen's marriage shows undiminished power. Here and there, perhaps, we have a little too much psychological analysis; but, after all, the reader who objects to psychology can avoid it by skipping a paragraph or two. It is another version of the old tragic motive: the paralysing influence of unmitigated and concentrated selfishness, already illustrated by Tito and Rosamond. Grandcourt, to whom Gwendolen sacrifices herself, is compared to a crab or a boa-constrictor slowly pinching its victim to death: to appeal to him for mercy would be as idle as to appeal to 'a dangerous serpent orna-mentally coiled on her arm.' He is a Tito in a further stage of development —with all better feelings atrophied, and enabled, by his fortune, to gratify his spite without exerting himself in intrigues. Like Tito, he suggests, to me at least, rather the cruel woman than the male autocrat. Some critic remarked, to George Eliot's annoyance, that the scenes between him and his parasite Lush showed 'the imperious feminine, not the masculine character'. She comforted herself by the statement that Bernal Osborne—a thorough man of the world—had commended these scenes as specially lifelike. I can, indeed, accept both views, for the distinction is rather too delicate for definite application. One feels, I think, that Grandcourt was drawn by a woman: but a sort of volup-tuous enjoyment of malignant tyranny is unfortunately not confined to either sex. Anyhow, Gwendolen's ordeal is pathetic, and she excites more sympathy than any of George Eliot's victims. Perhaps she excites a little too much. At least, when she comes very near homicide (like Caterina in the *Clerical Scenes* and Bulstrode in *Middlemarch*), and withholds her hand from her drowning husband, one is strongly tempted to give the verdict 'Served him right'. She, however, feels some remorse; and Daniel Deronda, who becomes her confessor, is much too admirable a being to give any sanction to this immoral source of consolation. She is so charming in her way that we feel more interest in the criminal than in the confessor. 'I have no sympathy', she says on one occasion 'with women who are always doing right'. Perhaps this is the reason why we cannot quite bow the knee before Daniel Deronda. . . .

I must repeat that George Eliot was intensely feminine, though more philosophical than most women. She shows it to the best purpose in the subtlety and the charm of her portraits of women, unrivalled in some ways by any writer of either sex; and shows it also, as I think, in a true perception of the more feminine aspects of her male characters. Still, she sometimes illustrates the weakness of the feminine view. Daniel Deronda is not merely a feminine but, one is inclined to say, a school-girl's hero. He is so sensitive and scrupulously delicate that he will not soil his hands by joining in the rough play of ordinary political and social reformers. He will not compromise, and yet he shares the dislike of his creator for fanatics and the devotees of 'fads'. The monomaniac type is certainly disagreeable, though it may be useful. Deronda con-trives to avoid its more offensive peculiarities but at the price of devoting himself to an unreal and dreamy object. Probably, one fancies he became disgusted in later life by finding that, after Mordecai's death, the people with whom he had to work had not the charm of that half-inspired visionary. He is, in any case, an idealist, who can only be provided with a task by a kind of providential interposition. The discovery that one can be carrying out one's grandfather's ideas is not generally a very

powerful source of information. 'Heredity' represents an important
factor in life, but can hardly be made into a religion. So far, therefore as
Deronda is an aesthetic embodiment of an ethical revelation—a
judicious hint to a young man in search of an ideal—he represents
an untenable theory. From the point of view of the simple novel reader
he fails from unreality. George Eliot in later years, came to know several
representatives in the younger generation of the class to which Deronda
belonged. She speaks, for example, with great warmth of Henry Sidg-
wick. His friends she remarks by their own account always 'expected
him to act according to a higher standard', higher than they would attribute to anyone else or adopt for themselves. She sent Deronda to
Cambridge soon after she had written this, and took great care to give
an accurate account of the incidents of Cambridge life. I have always
fancied—though without any evidence—that some touches of
Deronda were drawn from one of her friends, Edmund Gurney, a
man of remarkable charm of character and as good looking as Deronda.
In the Cambridge atmosphere of Deronda's days there was, I think, a
certain element of rough commonsense which might have rocked
some of her heroes' nonsense out of him. But, in any case, one is sensible
that George Eliot, if she is thinking of real life at all, has come to see
through a romantic haze which deprives the portrait of reality. The
imaginative sense is declining, and the characters are becoming emblems
or symbols of principle, and composed of more moonshine than solid
flesh and blood. The Gwendolen story taken by itself is a masterly piece
of social satire; but in spite of the approval of learned Jews, it is
impossible to feel any enthusiastic regard for Deronda in his
surroundings.

From *George Eliot* 1902, pp. 155–7, 167–71, 183–7, 190–1.

HENRY JAMES: 1908
A Weakness of Sympathy

I have . . . a weakness of sympathy with that constant effort of George
Eliot's which plays, through Adam Bede and Felix Holt and Tito Melema
through Daniel Deronda and through Lydgate in *Middlemarch*,
through Maggie Tulliver, through Romola, through Dorothea Brooke
and Gwendolen Harleth; the effort to show their adventures and their
history—the author's subject-matter all—as determined by their feelings
and the nature of their minds. Their emotions, their stirred intelligence,
their moral consciousness, become thus, by sufficiently charmed perusal,
our own very adventure. The creator of Deronda and of Romola is
charged, I know, with having on occasion—as in dealing with those
very celebrities themselves—left the figure, the concrete man and
woman, too abstract by reason of the quantity of soul employed; but
such mischances, where imagination and humour still keep them

company, often have an interest that is wanting to agitations of the mere surface or to those that may be only taken for granted. I should even like to give myself the pleasure of retracing from one of my own productions to another the play of like instinctive disposition, of catching in the fact, at one point after another, from *Roderick Hudson* to *The Golden Bowl* that provision for interest which consists in placing advantageously, placing right in the middle of the light, the most polished of possible mirrors of the subject. . . .

From the Preface to *The Princess Casamassima*, *The Novels and Tales of Henry James*, The New York Edition, 1908, Vol. 5, p. xv.

VIRGINIA WOOLF: 1919
A Centenary Assessment

To read George Eliot attentively is to become aware how little one knows about her. It is also to become aware of the credulity, not very creditable to one's insight, with which, half consciously and partly maliciously, one had accepted the late Victorian version of a deluded woman who held phantom sway over subjects even more deluded than herself. At what moment and by what means her spell was broken it is difficult to ascertain. Some people attribute it to the publication of her Life.[4] Perhaps George Meredith with his phrase about the 'mercurial little showman' and the 'errant woman' on the dais gave point and poison to the arrows of thousands incapable of aiming them so accurately but delighted to let fly. She became one of the butts for youth to laugh at, the convenient symbol of a group of serious people who were all guilty of the same idolatry and could be dismissed with the same scorn. Lord Acton had said that she was greater than Dante. Herbert Spencer exempted her novels, as if they were not novels, when he banned all fiction from the London Library. . . .

In fiction, where so much of personality is revealed, the absence of charm is a great lack; and her critics, who have been, of course, mostly of the opposite sex, have resented, half consciously perhaps, her deficiency in a quality which is held to be supremely desirable in women. George Eliot was not charming; she was not strongly feminine; she had none of those eccentricities and inequalities of temper which give to so many artists the endearing simplicity of children. One feels that to most people, as to Lady Ritchie, she was 'not exactly a personal friend, but a good and benevolent impulse'. But if we consider these portraits more closely we shall find that they are all the portraits of an elderly celebrated woman, dressed in black satin, driving in her victoria, a woman who has been through her struggle and issued from it with a profound desire to be of use to others, but with no wish for intimacy

[4] J. W. Cross, *George Eliot's Life as Related in her Letters and Journals*, 3 vols, 1885 (Ed.).

save with the little circle who had known her in the days of her youth. We know very little about the days of her youth; but we do know that the culture, the philosophy, the fame, and the influence were all built upon a very humble foundation—she was the granddaughter of a carpenter.

The first volume of her life is a singularly depressing record. In it we see her raising herself with groans and struggles from the intolerable boredom of petty provincial society (her father had risen in the world and become more middle class, but less picturesque) to be the assistant editor of a highly intellectual London review, and the esteemed companion of Herbert Spencer. The stages are painful as she reveals them in the sad soliloquy in which Mr. Cross condemned her to tell the story of her life. Marked in early youth as one 'sure to get something up very soon in the way of a clothing club,' she proceeded to raise funds for restoring a church by making a chart of ecclesiastical history; and that was followed by a loss of faith which so disturbed her father that he refused to live with her. Next came the struggle with the translation of Strauss, which, dismal and 'soul-stupefying' in itself, can scarcely have been made less so by the usual feminine tasks of ordering a household and nursing a dying father, and the distressing conviction, to one so dependent upon affection, that by becoming a blue-stocking she was forfeiting her brother's respect. 'I used to go about like an owl,' she said, 'to the great disgust of my brother.' 'Poor thing,' wrote a friend who saw her toiling through Strauss with a statue of the risen Christ in front of her, 'I do pity her sometimes with her pale sickly face and dreadful headaches, and anxiety, too, about her father.' Yet, though we cannot read the story without a strong desire that the stages of her pilgrimage might have been made, if not more easy, at least more beautiful, there is a dogged determination in her advance upon the citadel of culture which raises it above our pity. Her development was very slow and very awkward, but it had the irresistible impetus behind it of a deep-seated and noble ambition. Every obstacle at length was thrust from her path. She knew everyone. She read everything. Her astonishing intellectual vitality had triumphed. Youth was over, but youth had been full of suffering. Then, at the age of thirty-five, at the height of her powers, and in the fullness of her freedom, she made the decision which was of such profound moment to her and still matters even to us, and went to Weimar, alone with George Henry Lewes.

The books which followed so soon after her union testify in the fullest manner to the great liberation which had come to her with personal happiness. In themselves they provide us with a plentiful feast. Yet at the threshold of her literary career one may find in some of the circumstances of her life influences that turned her mind to the past, to the country village, to the quiet and beauty and simplicity of childish memories and away from herself and the present. We understand how it was that her first book was *Scenes of Clerical Life*, and not *Middlemarch*. Her union with Lewes had surrounded her with affection, but in view of the circumstances and of the conventions it had also isolated her. 'I wish it to be understood,' she wrote in 1857, 'that I should never invite anyone to come and see me who did not ask for the invitation.' She had been 'cut off from what is called the world,' she said later, but she did not regret it. By becoming thus marked, first by circumstances and later, inevitably, by her fame, she lost the power to move on equal terms unnoted among her kind; and the loss for a novelist was serious. Still, basking in the light and sunshine of *Scenes of Clerical Life*, feeling the large mature mind spreading itself with a luxurious sense of freedom in the world of her 'remotest past', to speak of loss seems inappropriate. Everything to such a mind was gain. All experience filtered down through layer after layer of perception and reflection, enriching and nourishing. The utmost we can say, in qualifying her attitude towards fiction by what little we know of her life, is that she had taken to heart certain lessons not usually learnt early, if learnt at all, among which perhaps the most branded upon her was the melancholy virtue of tolerance; her sympathies are with the everyday lot, and play most happily in dwelling upon the homespun of ordinary joys and sorrows. She has none of that romantic intensity which is connected with a sense of one's own individuality, unsated and unsubdued, cutting its shape sharply upon the background of the world. What were the loves and sorrows of a snuffy old clergyman, dreaming over his whisky, to the fiery egotism of Jane Eyre?

The beauty of those first books, *Scenes of Clerical Life*, *Adam Bede*, *The Mill on the Floss*, is very great. It is impossible to estimate the merit of the Poysers, the Dodsons, the Gilfils, the Bartons, and the rest with all their surroundings and dependencies, because they have put on flesh and blood and we move among them, now bored, now sympathetic, but always with that unquestioning acceptance of all that they say and do which we accord to the great originals only. The flood of memory and humour which she pours so spontaneously into one figure, one scene after another, until the whole fabric of ancient rural England is revived, has so much in common with a natural process that it leaves us with little consciousness that there is anything to criticize. We accept; we expand; we feel the delicious warmth and release of spirit which the great creative writers alone procure for us. As one comes back to the books after years of absence they pour out, even against our expectation, the same store of energy and heat, so that we want more than anything to idle in the warmth as in the sun beating down from the red orchard wall. If there is an element of unthinking abandonment in thus submitting to the humours of Midland farmers and their wives, that, too, is right in the circumstances. We scarcely wish to analyse what we feel to be so largely and deeply human. And when we consider how distant the world of Shepperton and Hayslope is, and how remote the minds of farmers and agricultural labourers from those of most of George Eliot's readers, we can only attribute the ease and pleasure with which we ramble from farmhouse

to smithy, from cottage parlour to rectory garden, to the fact that George
Eliot makes us share their lives not in a spirit of condescension or of
curiosity but in a spirit of sympathy. She is no satirist. The movement
of her mind was too slow and cumbersome to lend itself to comedy.
But she gathers in her large grasp a great bunch of the main elements of
human nature and groups them loosely together with a tolerant and
wholesome understanding which, as one finds upon re-reading, has not
only kept her figures fresh and free but has given them an unexpected
hold upon our laughter and tears. There is the famous Mrs. Poyser.
It would have been easy to work her idiosyncrasies to death, and, as it
is, perhaps, George Eliot gets her laugh in the same place a little too
often. But memory, after the book is shut, brings out, as sometimes in
real life, the details and subtleties which some more salient characteristic has prevented us from noticing at the time. We recollect that her
health was not good. There were occasions upon which she said nothing
at all. She was patience itself with a sick child. She doted upon Totty.
Thus one can muse and speculate about the greater number of George
Eliot's characters, and find, even in the least important, a roominess and
margin where those qualities lurk which she has no call to bring from
their obscurity.

But in the midst of all this tolerance and sympathy, there are, even in
the early books, moments of greater stress. Her humour has shown
itself broad enough to cover a wide range of fools and failures, mothers
and children, dogs and flourishing midland fields, farmers, sagacious
or fuddled over their ale, horse-dealers, inn-keepers, curates, and
carpenters. Over them all broods a certain romance, the only romance
that George Eliot allowed herself—the romance of the past. The books
are astonishingly readable and have no trace of pomposity or pretence.
But to the reader who holds a large stretch of her early work in view it
will become obvious that the mist of recollection gradually withdraws.
It is not that her power diminishes, for, to our thinking, it is at its
highest in the mature *Middlemarch*. But the world of fields and farms
no longer contents her. In real life she had sought her fortunes elsewhere; and though to look back into the past was calming and consoling,
there are, even in the early works, traces of that troubled spirit, that
exacting and questioning and baffled presence who was George Eliot
herself. In *Adam Bede* there is a hint of her in Dinah. She shows herself
far more openly and completely in Maggie in the *Mill on the Floss*. She
is Janet in 'Janet's Repentance', and Romola, and Dorothea seeking
wisdom and finding one scarcely knows what in marriage with Ladislaw.
Those who fall foul of George Eliot do so, we incline to think, on
account of her heroines; and with good reason; for there is no doubt
that they bring out the worst of her, lead her into difficult places, make
her self-conscious, didactic and occasionally vulgar. Yet if you could
delete the whole sisterhood you would leave a much smaller and a
much inferior world, albeit a world of greater artistic perfection and far
superior jollity and comfort. In accounting for her failure, in so far as it

was a failure, one recollects that she never wrote a story until she was thirty-seven, and that by the time she was thirty-seven she had come to think of herself with a mixture of pain and something like resentment. For long she preferred not to think of herself at all. Then, when the first flush of creative energy was exhausted and self-confidence had come to her, she wrote more and more from the personal standpoint, but she did so without the unhesitating abandonment of the young. Her self-consciousness is always marked when her heroines say what she herself would have said. She disguised them in every possible way. She granted them beauty and wealth into the bargain; she invented, more improbably, a taste for brandy. But the disconcerting and stimulating fact remained that she was compelled by the very power of her genius to step forth in person upon the quiet buccolic scene.

The noble and beautiful girl who insisted upon being born into the Mill on the Floss is the most obvious example of the ruin which a heroine can strew about her. Humour controls her and keeps her lovable so long as she is small and can be satisfied by eloping with the gipsies or hammering nails into her doll; but she develops; and before George Eliot knows what has happened she has a full-grown woman on her hands demanding what neither gipsies nor dolls, nor St. Ogg's itself is capable of giving her. First Philip Wakem is produced, and later Stephen Guest. The weakness of the one and the coarseness of the other have often been pointed out; but both, in their weakness and coarseness, illustrate not so much George Eliot's inability to draw the portrait of a man, as the uncertainty, the infirmity, and the fumbling which shook her hand when she had to conceive a fit mate for a heroine. She is in the first place driven beyond the home world she knew and loved, and forced to set foot in middle-class drawing rooms where young men sing all the summer morning and young women sit embroidering smoking caps for bazaars. She feels herself out of her element, as her clumsy satire of what she calls 'good society' proves.

"Good society has its claret and its velvet carpets, its dinner engagements six weeks deep, its opera, and its faëry ball rooms . . . gets its science done by Faraday and its religion by the superior clergy who are to be met in the best houses; how should it have need of belief and emphasis?"

There is no trace of humour or insight there, but only the vindictiveness of a grudge which we feel to be personal in its origin. But terrible as the complexity of our social system is in its demands upon the sympathy and discernment of a novelist straying across the boundaries, Maggie Tulliver did worse than drag George Eliot from her natural surroundings. She insisted upon the introduction of the great emotional scene. She must love; she must despair; she must be drowned clasping her brother in her arms. The more one examines the great emotional scenes the more nervously one anticipates the brewing and gathering and thickening of the clouds which will burst upon our heads at the moment of crisis in a shower of disillusionment and verbosity. It is

E

partly that her hold upon dialogue, when it is not dialect, is slack; and partly that she seems to shrink with an elderly dread of fatigue from the effort of emotional concentration. She allows her heroines to talk too much. She has little verbal felicity. She lacks the unerring taste which chooses one sentence and compresses the heart of the scene within that. 'Whom are you going to dance with?' asked Mr. Knightley at the Westons' ball. 'With you, if you will ask me,' said Emma; and she had said enough. Mrs. Casaubon would have talked for an hour and we should have looked out the window.

Yet, dismiss the heroines without sympathy, confine George Eliot to the agricultural world of her 'remotest past,' and you not only diminish her greatness but lose her true flavour. That greatness is hers we can have no doubt. The width of the prospect, the large strong outlines of the principal features, the ruddy light of the early books, the searching power and reflective richness of the later, tempt us to linger and expatiate beyond our limits. But it is upon the heroines that we would cast a final glance. 'I have always been finding out my religion since I was a little girl,' says Dorothea Casaubon. 'I used to pray so much—now I hardly ever pray. I try not to have desires merely for myself. . . .' She is speaking for them all. That is their problem. They cannot live without religion, and they start out on the search for one when they are little girls. Each has the deep feminine passion for good-ness, which makes the place where she stands, in aspiration and agony, the heart of the book—still and cloistered like a place of worship, but that she no longer knows to whom to pray. In learning they seek their goal; in the ordinary tasks of womanhood; in the wider service of their kind. They do not find what they seek, and we cannot wonder. The ancient consciousness of woman, charged with suffering and sensi-bility, and for so many ages dumb, seems in them to have brimmed and overflowed and uttered a demand for something—they scarcely know what—for something that is perhaps incompatible with the facts of human existence. George Eliot has far too strong an intelligence to tamper with those facts, or to mitigate the truth because it was a stern one. Save for the supreme courage of their endeavour, the struggle ends, for her heroines, in tragedy, or in a compromise that is even more melancholy. But their story is the incomplete version of the story of George Eliot herself. For her, too, the burden and the complexity of womanhood were not enough; she must reach beyond the sanctuary and pluck for herself the strange bright fruits of art and knowledge. Clasping them, as few women have ever clasped them, she would not renounce her own inheritance—the difference of view, the difference of standard—nor accept an inappropriate reward. Thus we behold her, a memorable figure, inordinately praised and shrinking from her fame, despondent, reserved, shuddering back into the arms of love as if there alone were satisfaction and, it might be, justification; at the same time reaching out with 'a fastidious yet hungry ambition, for all that life could offer the free and inquiring mind and confronting her feminine aspirations with the real world of men. Triumphant was the issue for her, whatever it may have been for her creations; and as we recollect all that she dared and achieved, how, crushed by sorrow, she mastered even that desolation and sought more knowledge and more understanding till the body, weighted with its double burden, sank and died worn out, we must lay upon her grave whatever we have in our power to bestow of laurel and rose.

From an unsigned article 'George Eliot', *Times Literary Supplement*, 20 November 1919, pp. 657–8.

J. W. BEACH: 1932
'Something Lying Deeper in the Consciousness'

. . . George Eliot often goes behind the apparent motive to something lying deeper in the consciousness which is the main determinant of conduct . . . it was in *Middlemarch* that George Eliot did her most remarkable work in this line. She had evidently been studying the science of psychology as it then existed, and was not unaware of the light to be thrown on psychological processes from the study of physiology. Most interesting is her analysis of the mental processes of Mr. Bulstrode. He is a wealthy banker of a deep and sincere religious faith, whose fortune was founded in a dishonest line of business and diverted to him from the person who should rightly have inherited it. He is not a plain hypocrite, but at all stages of his career has been obliged to persuade himself that what he was doing was really to the glory of God. This process of 'rationalizing', as we should now call it, is carefully analysed in chapter LXI, for example.

Then at a certain point in the story there turns up a drunken character named Raffles. He is the only one who knows of Bulstrode's wrongdoing, and is capable of exposing him to his wife and the whole countryside. Bulstrode is compelled to tell some lies to prevent his wife's learning the facts from Raffles, and this is a cause of great distress to him.

'For Bulstrode shrank from a direct lie with an intensity disproportionate to the number of his more indirect misdeeds. But many of these misdeeds were like the *subtle muscular movements which are not taken account of in the consciousness*, though they bring about the end that we fix our mind on and desire. And it is only what we are vividly conscious of that we can vividly imagine to be seen by Omniscience.'

Here is a notion, wherever George Eliot picked it up, strongly suggestive, not merely of a psychology well aware of the physiological bases of behaviour, but also of the Freudian theory of the Unconscious. This notion is more or less carried through in the account of the spiritual predicament in which Bulstrode now finds himself. It would be greatly to his interest if Raffles were dead. And Raffles is now in Bulstrode's house critically ill. Dr. Lydgate has specially warned against his being given any alcoholic stimulant. And Bulstrode cannot help thinking how fortunate it would be if Raffles were given something to drink and put out of the way. It is now that the doctor makes a visit, and Bulstrode has an opportunity to make a favourable impression on him by agreeing to assist in a hospital project which Lydgate has much at heart.

He did not measure the quantity of diseased motive which had made him wish for Lydgate's good-will, but the quantity was none the less actively there, like an irritating agent in his blood. A man vows, and yet will not cast away the means of breaking his vow. Is it that he distinctly means to break it? Not at all; but *the desires which tend to break it are at work in him dimly, and make their way into his imagination, and relax his muscles in the very moments when he is telling himself* over again the reasons for his vow. Raffles, recovering quickly, returning to the free use of his odious powers—how could Bulstrode wish for that? Raffles dead was the image that brought release, and indirectly he prayed for that way of release, beseeching that, if it were possible, the rest of his days here below might be freed from the threat of an ignominy which would break him utterly as an instrument of God's service.'

And so in the end it is the image of Raffles dead that wins out over the intention to do right, and Bulstrode connives at the carelessness of the nurse who does give Raffles his much desired alcoholic stimulant.

'The desires which tend to break [his vow] are at work in him dimly.' Here again is an expression that suggests the modern theory of the Unconscious. . . .

From *The Twentieth Century Novel: Studies in Technique*, New York: The Century Company, 1932, pp. 30–2.

T. S. ELIOT: 1953
Rosamond

(And I am quite sure that Rosamond Vincy, in *Middlemarch*, frightens me far more than Goneril or Regan.) It seems to me that what happens, when an author creates a vital sort of character, is a sort of give-and-take. The author may put into that character. . . . Something perhaps never realized in his own life. . . .

From 'The Three Voices of Poetry', 1953, *On Poetry and Poets*, 1957, Faber, pp. 94–3.

Modern Critics on
George Eliot

JEROME BEATY

Middlemarch: The Writing of
Chapter 81

There are no revisions at all on the first manuscript page of chapter 81.[1]
An unrevised page is so unusual in George Eliot's manuscript of
Middlemarch that one is immediately inclined either to believe Cross's
version of the inspired writing of this chapter[2] or to suspect that the
page had been rewritten. The last line of the page appears in the bottom
margin, often a sign that George Eliot was rewriting a page and spacing
it to meet an already completed one. The motto at the head of the
chapter clearly was added at a later time: unlike the rest of the page it is
in violet ink and spaced two written lines to each ruled line.

With the end of page 91 the lack of revision ends. The next page[3]
contains a number of individually rather minor changes. In the very
first sentence, Lydgate's rather pompous 'one'—'When one is grateful
... one does not'—is changed to the regal 'we' and changed back again.
In the next paragraph, 'suddenly doubting' has been substituted for
'checked by [word illegible] doubt' because 'cheque' appears in the
next sentence: 'Yes, the cheque is going to Bulstrode today.' Similar
revisions toward the end of the page avoid repetition of 'surprise.'
There are a number of other minor changes on this page, as there are
throughout the chapter, which shall not be discussed for lack of space

[1] Page ends 3: 396, 'her into the drawing-room, he.'

[2] 'George Eliot ... told me that, in all that she considered her best writing,
there was a "not herself" which took possession of her, and that she felt her own
personality to be merely the instrument through which this spirit, as it were,
was acting. Particularly she dwelt on this in regard to the scene in "Middlemarch" between Dorothea and Rosamond, saying that, although she always
knew they had, sooner or later, to come together, she kept the idea resolutely
out of her mind until Dorothea was in Rosamond's drawing-room. Then,
abandoning herself to the inspiration of the moment, she wrote the whole
scene exactly as it stands, without alteration or erasure, in an intense state of
excitement and agitation, feeling herself entirely possessed by the feelings of
the two women.' (Cross, *Life*, 1885, 3, 424–5) [Quoted Beaty, p. 106].

[3] Page ends 3: 399, 'she coloured and gave rather a.'

On page 92, however, one change at least is substantial: 'He [Lydgate] had told her of Dorothea's letter containing the cheque, and afterwards' has been inserted in the manuscript, so that in the new version Rosamond is prepared for her confession by being immediately put consciously in Dorothea's debt. Preparation for Rosamond's confession accounts for other relatively important changes. We first see Rosamond in this chapter as she

sat languidly considering what she should do next, her natural industry in small things always[4] prompting her to begin some kind of occupation. . . .	sat languidly wondering what she should do next, her habitual industry in small things, even in the days of her sadness, prompting her to begin some kind of occupation. . . .[5]

The addition of 'wondering' and 'sadness' has a small but appreciable effect in turning our sympathies toward Rosamond, up to now—with all her selfish 'considering'—an object of our blame and hatred. The minor shift from 'natural' to 'habitual' keeps the point of view less than omniscient, keeps it outside Rosamond at this point; manipulation of point of view was an important factor in George Eliot's revision of this chapter.

The first half of page 93 has almost no revisions, and the rest of the pages contains only minor ones. A change in one sentence of Rosamond's dialogues[6] perhaps tones down her imperiousness, and a later change rephrases an awkwardly quoted thought, making it indirect and eliminating repetition of forms of 'trust'.

There are two beginnings for manuscript page 94. The first, clearly numbered '94', is a fifty-word passage on the back of the manuscript page of chapter 81 (p. 112):

sibility. Will had wounded her too sharply for her to feel any compunction towards him & Dorothea: she felt her own injury too keenly to feel theirs, & in the hour of her bruised pride she had been compelled to feel that her much offending husband was after all her best refuge.

The last four syllables of 'impossibility' which begin the earlier version of this page George Eliot inserted in the bottom margin of page 93; she thus began the new page 94 with 'Will.' Besides eliminating 'the hour of her bruised pride' and the repetitions of 'feel,' the new version represents a change in tactics: though we are at this point to sympathize

[4] 'Always' was first replaced by 'still,' then by the phrase in the right-hand column.
[5] The original version is on the left, the revised version on the right, here and throughout this extract. The original version is the MS. of *Middlemarch*, 4 vols., British Museum Additional Manuscripts 34,034–34,037. The revised version, and references in brackets on the right, is the 3 volume Cabinet Edition, Blackwood, 1878–80 (Ed.).
[6] From, ' "Tell Martha not to let any one else into the drawing-room," "Pray tell Martha not to bring any one else" ' etc.

with Rosamond to some extent, as the changes on page 92 indicate, and though in this chapter she is partially to atone for her sins, the shift from the hateful to the sympathetic Rosamond cannot be made too quickly—Rosamond must act with uncharacteristic selfishness only under the impact of Dorothea's own selflessness. This same consideration is perhaps responsible for many of the other revisions which stud the remainder of page 94:

Dorothea was not only the 'preferred' woman, but had also a formidable hold on Rosamond as a benefactor of her husband; [to] poor Rosamond's pained confused vision is seemed that this Mrs. Casaubon—this woman who predominated in all things concerning her—must have come to her with the sense of her advantage, and with an animosity that must make her desire to use it. Indeed, not Rosamond only, but any one else, knowing only the outer facts of the case, and not only the simple inspiration on which Dorothea acted, might well have wondered what she came for.

Looking likely [*sic*] the lovely ghost of herself, her graceful slimness wrapped in her soft white shawl, the rounded infant-like lips inevitably mild and innocent. Rosamond paused at three yards' distance from her visitor and bowed. But Dorothea, who had taken off her gloves, from an impulse which she could never resist when she wanted a sense of freedom, and looking with open sadness into Rosamond's[7] put out her hand. Rosamond could not avoid meeting her glance, could not avoid putting her little hand into Dorothea's, which clasped it with gentle motherliness; and

Dorothea was not only the 'preferred' woman, but had also a formidable advantage in being Lydgate's benefactor; and to poor Rosamond's pained confused vision it seemed that this Mrs. Casaubon —this woman who predominated in all things concerning her—must have come now with the sense of having the advantage, and with animosity prompting her to use it. Indeed, not Rosamond only, but any one else, knowing the outer facts of the case, and not the simple inspiration on which Dorothea acted, might well have wondered why she came.

Looking like the lovely ghost of herself, her graceful slimness wrapped in her soft white shawl, the rounded infantine mouth and cheek inevitably suggesting mildness and innocence, Rosamond paused at three yards' distance from her visitor and bowed. But Dorothea, who had taken off her gloves, from an impulse which she could never resist when she wanted a sense of freedom, came forward, and with her face full of a sad yet sweet openness, put out her hand. Rosamond could not avoid meeting her glance, could not avoid putting her small hand into Dorothea's, which clasped it with gentle

continued on page 62, column 1   *continued on page 62, column 2*

[7] The incomplete structure in this version apparently indicates that George Eliot made the revision in mid-sentence. Where this seems to be the case in passages quoted below, no notation will be made.

continued from page 61, column 1

immediately a doubt of her own prepossessions began to stir within her. Rosamond's eye was quick for faces; she saw Dorothea's face looked pale and changed since yesterday, yet gentle.

continued from page 61, column 2

motherliness; and immediately a doubt of her own prepossessions began to stir within her. Rosamond's eye was quick for faces; she saw Mrs. Casaubon's face looked pale and changed since yesterday, yet gentle (3: 398–9).

Related to the timing of Rosamond's confession is the delicate manipulation of point of view highlighted by the revision of this page. An important element in this chapter is the misunderstanding of each woman about the other: Rosamond thinks Dorothea has come to upbraid her or to gloat; Dorothea believes Will loves Rosamond. The omniscient reader knows all, but it is essential that he understand the feelings caused by each woman's limited knowledge of the other; the point of view thus shifts delicately from one of the women to the other and between internal and external views of them and of the situation. Up to the last sentence of the first paragraph on the page, events are seen through Rosamond's mind. There is a shift to an external viewer—'any one else'—but with an appeal to the omniscience of the reader: *we* know 'the simple inspiration on which Dorothea acted'. The beginning of the second paragraph maintains this external view—of what Rosamond looks like—though this may be seen through Dorothea's eyes, and the same ambivalent point of view is maintained through the explanation of Dorothea's impulse to remove her gloves; the view then moves outside Dorothea—to see Dorothea's look—on its way back to Rosamond: Rosamond 'could not avoid,' 'a doubt . . . began to stir within her.' Many of the revisions here, as in other passages in this chapter, may be attributed to these subtle shifts: e.g., the change from 'mild and innocent' to the carefully external 'suggesting mildness and innocence'[8] and the change from the too friendly and familiar 'Dorothea's face' to 'Mrs. Casaubon's face' which keeps the point of view Rosamond's.

The next manuscript page, 95, contains very few revisions, and most of these were made either during the writing of the sentence in which they appear or in proof. The last word of the page, 'deal,'[9] is in the bottom margin, perhaps an indication that this page was rewritten from an earlier version, though there is no other concrete evidence to this effect.

Page 96[10] contains few revisions, but some of these are rather extensive,[11] and one reveals a shift in tactics:

[8] George Eliot apparently made this change in proof, since the manuscript reads like the original. Bound proof of the first edition corrected by the author is in the possession of Wing Commander G. D. Blackwood, who very kindly permitted me to examine it, but proof of this chapter is missing.

[9] Page ends 3: 399, 'to know a great deal'.

[10] Page ends 3: 400, 'He confessed to me.'

[11] For example, the change from 'The cordial, pleading tones which seemed in this warm flow to be utterly heedless of,' to, 'The cordial, pleading tones which seemed to flow with generous heedlessness.'

Of course Mrs. Casaubon had the fact in her mind—she had been suffering—she loved [word illegible] Will [word illegible] words implied [he knew][12] it.

Of course Mrs. Casaubon had the facts in her mind, but she was not going to speak of anything connected with them.

The deleted passage dealt too directly with the Will–Dorothea situation, which George Eliot wanted to keep at this point as an undercurrent, not as a force on the surface of the action, so that Dorothea may not seem to be seeking a favour in exchange for her kindness and may not seem even to suspect that Rosamond has anything to tell her about Will. Both these changes, however, involve incomplete original passages, George Eliot making them while writing the very sentence in which they appear.

The first part of page 97[13], like the two pages preceding it, is relatively unrevised; Dorothea's speech, which makes up half the page, contains only a few minor changes. Revision of the next paragraph, however, is rather interesting.

Dorothea's face had become animated and as it beamed on Rosamond very close to her, she felt something like [awe] of a [supernatural] presence at this self-forgetful ardour in look and speech. Blushing she said, with embarassment, 'Thank you: you are very kind.'

Dorothea's face had become animated, and as it beamed on Rosamond very close to her, she felt something like bashful timidity before a superior, in the presence of this self-forgetful ardour. She said with blushing embarrassment, 'Thank you: you are very kind.'

If this reading of the almost illegible deleted passage is correct, the gist of the revision is clear: it tones down somewhat the already embarrassing adulation of Dorothea by the other characters in the novel (and by the author), and, in so far as it does, it improves the passage for those who find George Eliot's praise of her heroine excessive.

Extensive revision begins again about the middle of page 98. The opening paragraphs contain revisions only on the order of those on pages 95-7, but the paragraph which ends the page was significantly altered:

Rosamond felt her inward wound pang, as if a wound had been pierced, burst into crying as she had done the day before, and clung to Dorothea's arm [and must

continued on page 64, column 1

Rosamond, with a over-mastering pang, as if a wound within her had been probed, burst into hysterical crying as she had done the day before when she clung to her hus-

continued on page 64, column 2

---

[12] Square brackets enclose conjectural reading of partially legible words in the manuscript.

[13] Page ends 3: 401, 'that his misfortunes must'.

continued from page 63, column 1

have] [at least one word illegible] her husband's. Poor Dorothea was feeling a great wave of her sorrow returning over her as her thought was [word illegible] drawn to the possible share that Will Ladislaw might have in [any] Rosamond's mental tumult. She was beginning to fear that she should not be able to suppress herself enough to the end of this meeting, and while Rosamond was clinging to her, she was struggling against her own sobs.

continued from page 63, column 2

band. Poor Dorothea was feeling a great wave of her own sorrow returning over her—her thought being drawn to the possible share that Will Ladislaw might have in Rosamond's mental tumult. She was beginning to fear that she should not be able to suppress herself enough to the end of this meeting, and while her hand was still resting on Rosamond's lap, though the hand underneath it was withdrawn, she was struggling against her own rising sobs (3:402).

Though Rosamond is crying, even hysterical, she is not yet ready to reach out for Dorothea, to cling to her. Rosamond, like her hand, is as yet withdrawn.

Neither the paragraph nor the changes end with the end of page 98; page 99[14] begins:

She tried to master herself with the thought that this might be the turning-point in three lives—not her own; no, there the irrevocable had happened, but—in the lives of those three lives which were touching hers with the solemn neighbourhood of danger and distress. The fragile creature who was crying close to her—there might still be time to bring her back into the [confidence and faithfulness from] which she was [wandering] was unlike any other: she and Rosamond could never be together again with the same thrilling consciousness of yesterday within them both.

She tried to master herself with the thought that this might be the turning-point in three lives—not her own; no, there the irrevocable happened, but—in those three lives which were touching hers with the solemn neighbourhood of danger and distress. The fragile creature who was crying close to her—there might still be time to rescue her from the misery of false incompatible bonds; and this moment was unlike any other: she and Rosamond could never be together again with the same thrilling consciousness of yesterday within them both. She felt the relation between them to be peculiar enough to give her a peculiar influence, though she had no conception that the way in which her own feelings were involved was fully known to Mrs. Lydgate.

The purpose of lessening Rosamond's 'offence' at this point is not clear; to 'bring back' suggests an error already committed, to 'rescue one

[14] Page ends 3: 403, 'Pride was broken down between these two.'

which can still be avoided; escape from 'false incompatible bonds' is certainly more abstract and possibly less severe than a breach of 'confidence and faithfulness'. Perhaps it was to make Rosamond's atonement more conceivable, some preparation for it being necessary; perhaps it was to reveal, since this is a statement of what was in Dorothea's mind, that Dorothea, despite her better judgment, was still unwilling to believe what she thought she had seen the day before, and that she was hoping for an outcome like that which was indeed forthcoming. The long sentence which concludes this paragraph was written on the back of the page with a note to 'Insert' and on the front a note to 'Set Back,' a form of revision rare in George Eliot's manuscript. The sentence serves as a transition between Dorothea's point of view, which has dominated the paragraph from 'Poor Dorothea' (p. 98) and Rosamond's point of view, which dominates the next paragraph. It also helps explain why Dorothea feels free to go on with her advice: by specifying that Dorothea is ignorant of Rosamond's knowledge of the emotional relationship between Will and Dorothea, George Eliot makes her continuing both more credible and less hypocritical, for if Dorothea were aware that Rosamond knew of that relationship, her continuing would have been a conscious playing on the affections of Rosamond. That Dorothea is not doing so even now is hard to believe.

That neither woman truly understands the full extent either of the emotions or of the knowledge of the other is underlined once again in the next paragraph by the only other significant revisions on the page; George Eliot is describing Rosamond's reaction:

this strange unexpected manifestation of feeling in Dorothea a woman whom she had approached with a shrinking aversion and dread made her soul totter. . . .	this strange unexpected manifestation of feeling in a woman whom she had approached with a shrinking aversion and dread, as one who must necessarily have a jealous hatred towards her, made her soul totter. . . .

The deletion of 'Dorothea' emphasizes that Rosamond and Dorothea are still more or less strangers, and the added phrase emphasizes Rosamond's misunderstanding of what was going on in Dorothea's soul, Rosamond judging Dorothea by her own, or at least by human, standards.

George Eliot apparently rewrote completely some of the pages between 100 and 104: she changed page numbers and wrote words in the bottom margin. Exactly which pages she rewrote cannot be ascertained, but the three pages now numbered 100–102 seem to be second drafts of two earlier pages, 100–101. Since some of these pages, particularly the early ones, seem to have been rewritten, they naturally now contain but few revisions, and these are minor. But from the end of the first full paragraph on page 102 through Rosamond's confession of what had actually taken place between her and Will the day before—in some ways the heart of the chapter—there were frequent, extensive, and significant revisions, particularly in the description of how Rosamond speaks while confessing:

'You are thinking what is not true,' said Rosamond while she was still feeling Dorothea's arms round her—a necessity to free herself from something that oppressed her as if it were blood-guiltiness.

They moved apart, looking at each other.

'When you came in yesterday —it was not as you thought,' said Rosamond [in a low tone].

There was a movement of sur-surprised attention in Dorothea [word illegible]. She expected a vindication of Rosamond herself.

'He was telling me he loved another woman, [and] that I might know he could never love me. And now I think he hates me because— because you mistook him yester-day. He says it is through me that you will think ill of him—think that he is a false person. But it shall not be through me [which] [several words illegible] [bitter-ness],'—Rosamond now spoke with her utmost distinctness and determination. . . .

'You are thinking what is not true,' said Rosamond in an eager half-whisper, while she was still feeling Dorothea's arms round her—urged by a mysterious necessity to free herself from something that oppressed her as if it were blood-guiltiness.

They moved apart, looking at each other.

'When you came in yesterday —it was not as you thought,' said Rosamond in the same tone.

There was a movement of surprised attention in Dorothea. She expected a vindication of Rosa-herself.

'He was telling me he loved another woman, that I might know he could never love me,' said Rosamond, getting more and more hurried as she went on. 'And now I think he hates me because— because you mistook him yester-day. He says it is through me that you will think ill of him—think that he is a false person. But it shall not be through me' (3: 406)

What these revisions of stage directions constitute is not only a change in the tone of the passage but a deeper insight, or the presentation of that insight, into how a Rosamond would feel, speak, and act at this juncture. A scene in which the villain repents and thereby ensures the happiness of the hero and heroine is difficult to justify in any work demanding more *vraisemblance* than comedy. This scene requires just such a switch in the actions of a character hitherto presented as shallow, vain, and egocentric, incapable of imagining the feelings of others. How can George Eliot motivate such a change? How can she present it? The motivation she points out in paragraph following the confession:

"Rosamond had delivered her soul under impulses which she had not known before. She had begun her confession under the subduing influence of Dorothea's emotion; and as she went on she had gathered the sense that she was repelling Will's reproaches, which were still like a knife-wound within her."

In the original version of this scene, Rosamond, with Dorothea's arms around her, feels that it is necessary to confess, and when the women move apart, Rosamond's voice becomes more distinct and she becomes conscious of confessing, determined to go on. In the revised version, with the addition of the 'eager half-whisper' and 'mysterious' urge, the unconscious element of Rosamond's beginning to confess—she is under the influence of a stronger, deeper-feeling personality—is emphasized, and when the two women move apart Rosamond speaks not more determinedly, but more hastily; her confession was triggered by Dorothea's arms about her, by Dorothea's emotion, but, once she began, the memory of Will's accusations of the day before gave impetus to the confession and kept it pouring forth. The revisions, in other words, underline the unconsciousness of the impulse which makes Rosamond begin to tell the truth and motivates the latter part of the unburdening, still unconscious, by the remembered experience of Will's galling speech of the day before, which Rosamond, whose very vanity would cause her to store up this speech, has had festering within her. The revisions thus make the action justify the author's analysis which follows; that analysis perhaps caused the revision, George Eliot herself only growing aware of the motivation as she wrote it.

Revision of this delicately balanced confession scene continues at the bottom of page 102[15] and at the top of page 103[16], not, as before, in the description of Rosamond's tone, but in the substance of what she actually says:

". . . He has never had any love for me. He has always thought slightly of me. I imagined that he had some regard for me, but now I am sure that[17] he had none. He said yesterday that no other woman existed for him beside you. The blame of what happened is entirely mine. He said he could never explain to you—he is in despair. He said he would not sacrifice me—[about two words illegible] by telling you that I had shown my feeling too strongly.

". . . He has never had any love for me—I know he has not—he has always thought slightly of me. He said yesterday that no other woman existed for him beside you. The blame of what happened is entirely mine. He said he could never explain to you—because of me. He said you could never think well of him again. But now I have told you, and he cannot reproach me any more."

continued on page 68, column 1

[15] Page ends 3: 406, 'slightly of me. He said'.

[16] Page ends 3: 407, 'I was very unhappy. I am'.

[17] The phrase 'now I am sure that' was inserted before the entire passage was deleted.

continued from page 67, column 1

He is in despair because you will
never think well of him again.
But now I have told you, you will
and he cannot reproach me any
more."

The revised version does not merely gain in economy, but again, consciously or unconsciously, thoroughly realizes the character of Rosamond: even under the mysterious impulse, even with the promptings of a guilt feeling and the desire, based on her vanity, to negate the words Will flung at her the day before, even then, some of Rosamond's vanity and self-righteousness assert themselves—the revision eliminates three uses of 'I' in a blameworthy connection prior to the last self-congratulatory sentence and substitutes just one; it eliminates from her confession the facts that she imagined Will loved her and that she revealed her feelings about him. Rosamond still shoulders the blame, but what she is guilty of is stated in abstract terms, and in terms of Will's reaction (which caused this part of the confession in the first place) rather than in terms of her own actions or thoughts. Thus, even while rising far enough out of character to confess, Rosamond, in the revised passage, preserves enough of her own character to make the confession credible.

Other revisions on page 103 deal chiefly with Dorothea's reaction to confession:

she could only feel that this would be joy when she had recovered her power of feeling it. But she immediately [one or two words illegible] response to Rosamond's last words and said earnestly,

'No, he cannot reproach you any more.'

she could only perceive that this would be joy when she had recovered her power of feeling it. Her immediate consciousness was one of immense sympathy without check; she cared for Rosamond without struggle now, and responded earnestly to her last words—

'No, he cannot reproach you any more.'

With her usual tendency to overestimate the good in others, she felt a great outgoing of her heart towards Rosamond, for the generous effort which had redeemed her from suffering, not counting that the effort was a reflex of her own energy.[18]

[18] It is difficult to tell what, if any, of this paragraph was the first version of this page. From 'With' to 'great' may have been added in the space left by paragraphing—it begins immediately after 'more' with no new paragraph indicated; 'her from suffering, not count—' was added in the left margin of the manuscript page.

The sentence added to the first of these paragraphs reminds the reader that Dorothea's struggle with jealousy had not been finally won at dawn but has been continuing throughout her visit; up to this point she has been able to care for Rosamond only by force of will. Even though the extent of the revision of the last paragraph is not certain, its purpose seems clear: it gives almost all the credit for Rosamond's confession to Dorothea. If this change does help explain Rosamond's uncharacteristic generosity, it makes Dorothea's goodness almost unbearable—not all changes are improvements.

Revisions on page 104[19] and up to the last paragraph on page 105, the last paragraph of the chapter, are numerous but of relatively minor importance. Changes in the last paragraph, however, significantly alter the end of the chapter: Rosamond is speaking to Lydgate after Dorothea has left:

'I think she has,' said Rosamond.	'I think she has,' said Rosamond, looking up in his face.
'She told me that you said you would not do anything stay in Middlemarch[20] or do anything that I disliked.'	

The original version of the chapter ends here, but George Eliot, after revising the first sentence, wrote, apparently in several stages, a new ending:

'How heavy your eyes are, Tertius—and do push your hair back.' He lifted his large white hand to obey her, and felt thankful for this little mark of interest in him. Poor Rosamond's vagrant fancy had come back terribly scourged[21]—meek enough to nestle under the old despised shelter. And the shelter was still there: Lydgate had accepted his[22] narrowed lot with sad resignation. He had chosen this fragile creature, and had taken the burthen of her life upon his arms. He must walk as he could, carrying that burthen pitifully.

George Eliot wrote the first two sentences in the bottom margin and the rest of the passage on the back of the page. She wrote the inserted passage from 'Poor Rosamond's' on the back page, and from 'meek' on wrote the passage in violet ink, adding it, apparently, at a later date, perhaps when she was re-reading this portion of the novel before sending it off to the publisher. . . .

[19] Page ends 3: 408, 'order your carriage to come for you?'
[20] George Eliot inserted 'stay in Middlemarch' and perhaps deleted the first 'do anything' before deleting the entire passage.
[21] Deleted here in mid-sentence was, 'its bruised hope [word illegible] glad enough to nestle under'.
[22] The phrase 'accepted his' was substituted for 'endured with sad resignation', apparently in mid-sentence.

Chapter 81 thus was originally to have ended, ' "She told me that you said you would not do anything . . . that I disliked, " ' with the galling reassertion of Rosamond's vanity and egocentric single-mindedness, the interview with Dorothea and her experience of the day before having had no lasting effect on her at all. But this reversion to type was too swift and too complete. Rosamond could not be expected to change completely, but she had for the first time been compelled to look at life from a point of view not her own, and this experience must be allowed some influence, no matter how slight. In the bottom margin and on the back of the page George Eliot devised a new ending: Rosamond has been affected by her experiences with Will and Dorothea; she has been forced to return to her husband's protection and in some measure to appreciate it. But she still is Rosamond enough to make even her tenderness a form of domination—' ". . . do push your hair back." ' George Eliot also added Lydgate's reaction: his resignation, his shortening of the lines of his experience. This, too, changes the tone. Had George Eliot not revised, the chapter would have ended on a note of shrill hatred for Rosamond and of disgust with Lydgate for not asserting himself once and for all. It now ends quite differently, on a note of pity for both Lydgates, almost like that pity we felt earlier in the novel (chapter 74) for the Bulstrodes when Harriet stood beside her husband, as Lydgate, in a somewhat similar gesture, now stands beside his wife.

That George Eliot was inspired when she wrote chapter 81 of *Middlemarch* may well be true, but that 'she kept the idea' of this chapter 'resolutely out of her mind until Dorothea was in Rosamond's drawing-room' is contradicted by her notebook, and that 'she wrote the whole scene exactly as it stands, without alteration or erasure' is contradicted by the manuscript of the novel.

George Eliot's Quarry for 'Middlemarch'[23] reveals that she considered several possible occasions for the scene, that she concerned herself in advance with defining Dorothea's motive in coming to see Rosamond and Rosamond's in confessing, and that she had the main ideas of the chapter in mind before she began writing it.

The manuscript reveals that the author made some changes while writing, others later when she was reading the manuscript over, and still others when reading proof. She changed a word, a phrase, a sentence, or a passage. She added passages on the backs of pages. She rewrote whole pages, groups of consecutive pages. She made changes in every stage of writing and of almost every possible extent.

She made changes in matters of style and changes in the matter itself. Chief among the latter were those made necessary by the need for careful timing, presentation, and motivation of Rosamond's out-of-

[23] A. T. Kitchel (ed.), *George Eliot's Quarry for 'Middlemarch'*, University of California Press, Berkeley and Los Angeles, 1950. And see J. C. Pratt, *A Middlemarch Miscellany. An Edition With Introduction and Notes of George Eliot's 1868–1871 Notebook*. (Unpublished Ph.D. Princeton University 1965), [Ed. Note].

character speech. George Eliot had also to manipulate the point of view very carefully and subtly, shifting it delicately back and forth between the two women, a manipulation which necessitated careful revision. Finally, she revised the tone of the end of the chapter, changing Rosamond's too quick and total reversion to hateful type to show her scarred, if still selfish, together with her husband an object of pity as well as blame.

So this chapter, which, according to Cross, George Eliot herself identified as having been written spontaneously and without change, was, in fact, prepared for with reasonable care and was revised in all stages of its evolution and in almost all its aspects; timing, content, point of view, characterization, tone, and outcome. Writing, to George Eliot, was not an unpremeditated outpouring; neither was it a mechanical following of detailed blueprint. It was a process of evolution and of discovery.

The beginning of *Middlemarch* flowed together from its twin sources in the earlier 'Middlemarch' and 'Miss Brooke'. The amount of plot material on hand after this joining required more space than the conventional three-decker could afford, and to suit this need Lewes originated the half-volume parts form, which form in turn made demands upon the novel and dictated certain changes in its nature. When the novel was well under way but progress was still uncertain, George Eliot paused to sketch out plans for the last five parts in her notebook, and she continued to use the notebook to outline portions of the novel, block off parts, study relationships of one plot line to the other, and otherwise prepare the scaffolding for the last portion of the novel. She was not a slave to her own plans, however; she changed them even as she wrote when new relationships and developments impossible to anticipate revealed themselves. And throughout this process, throughout the writing of the novel—even in chapter 81 but not peculiarly or particularly in that chapter—she made changes. These revisions, both of plan and of the words already written, which George Eliot made while writing and even after writing, give a depth and richness to the novel which no mechanical adherence to outline could have done. In this writing process such terms as 'spontaneous' and 'contrived,' 'conscious' or 'unconscious' have no meaning. The whole being, the artist, struggles with his medium, words, and through them both expresses and discovers what he has to say. What, in 1869–72, George Eliot had to say is *Middlemarch*.

From Jerome Beaty, *Middlemarch from Notebook to Novel: A Study of George Eliot's Creative Method*, The University of Illinois Press Urbana, 1960, pp. 111–23.

DAVID DAICHES:

George Eliot

. . . Before George Eliot . . . the English novel had been almost entirely the work of those whose primary purpose was to entertain. Not that earlier novelists had lacked moral purpose; Richardson 'taught the passions to move at the command of virtue', and something similar might have been said of Goldsmith in his *Vicar of Wakefield*. Of Thackeray's moral feeling we are never left long in doubt and Dickens, too, worked within a clearly suggested framework of values. Nevertheless, no English novelist from Defoe to Thackeray could have been called a man of great philosophical powers and unusual erudition; their presentation of the human scene was never in any degree conditioned by the depth of their intellectual penetration or the profundity of their moral speculations, still less by the vastness of their learning. They were content to follow the patterns of thought of their day and to handle ideas only obliquely and symbolically. Their job was to construct stories—moving, edifying, entertaining, or something of all three—not to exhibit new ideas. It was the poets, not the novelists, who in England traditionally moved in the intellectual vanguard (though even the poets were rarely intellectual pioneers). From Fulke Greville to Wordsworth there had always been poets to present poetically new notions of man and the world; the novelists—to put the matter bluntly —were as a rule less well educated. George Eliot was the first English novelist to move in the vanguard of the thought and learning of her day, and in doing so added new scope and dignity to the English novel. . . .

The sentimentality of Dickens and the intrusive moral platitudinizing —equally sentimental in its way—of Thackeray derive at bottom from a lack of intelligence. Unable to accept simple supernatural sanctions for morality, these writers found no alternative except a facile appeal to 'feeling' and as a result were unable to cope convincingly with the really disturbing moral problems—the suffering or death of a good character, for example. George Eliot, who was both idealist and agnostic and derived both her idealism and her agnosticism from her own intellectual inquiries into moral and religious questions, had her own answer to these difficulties; she was too intelligent ever to try to solve a moral problem by mere sentimentality. One might quote again from F. W. H. Myers' record of a conversation he had with George Eliot at Cambridge in 1873: '. . . she, stirred somewhat beyond her wont, and taking as her text the three words which have been used so often as the inspiring trumpet-calls of men—the words *God, Immortality, Duty*—pronounced, with terrible earnestness, how inconceivable was the *first*, how unbelievable the *second*, and yet how peremptory and absolute the *third*'. This mixture of idealism and astringency, which may sound rather terrifying in straight philosophical discourse, can be a great source of strength when transmuted into terms of characters 'doing and suffering' in a novel. It can enable irony and tenderness to coexist, as they do in *Adam Bede*; it can produce the kind of humour which manifests itself in the portrayal of the scatterbrained but not unsympathic Mr. Brooke of *Middlemarch* and the relentless analysis of the dilemma and the deterioration of Dr. Lydgate in the same novel; it can make possible that impressive combination of censure and sympathy with which Gwendolyn Harleth is presented in *Daniel Deronda*. At the same time, that 'terrible earnestness' can produce the unbelievable and oracular virtuousness of Daniel Deronda himself and of Felix Holt in the novel of that name, and is responsible, too, for the note of excessive idealization which occasionally obtrudes itself in even the best of her novels.

In all her fiction, George Eliot was concerned with moral problems of character, but she never abstracted her characters from their environment in order to illustrate their moral dilemmas. She was familiar with and responsive to the varied social contexts in which nineteenth-century men and women could live; she saw the relationship between town and country, between landed families living in an ever-diminishing feudal atmosphere and neighbouring provincial towns where farmer and tradesman, banker and politician, jostled each other in a world of perpetually intersecting interests. She knew England, both town and country, metropolitan and provincial, agricultural, commercial, industrial, and professional, and she used her knowledge to make her characters move naturally in their daily occupations . . . what English novelist before George Eliot took men's daily occupations seriously? From the *Canterbury Tales* onward, the English tradition was to show people on holiday and to refer to their trades or professions merely as background. But George Eliot's Dr. Lydgate is a doctor with real medical problems, and she reports his discussion of them accurately; we are told precisely the subject of Mr. Casaubon's research (in *Middlemarch*) and precisely wherein it is lacking; the agricultural activity of the Poysers in *Adam Bede* is presented fully and convincingly with a wealth of detail; and so throughout all the novels. Further, these pictures of men at work are intimately bound up with her presentation of character and of the moral problems of character. It is the relationships into which people are brought in the course of their daily activities that precipitate the changes and the crises out of which the ultimate moral meaning emerges. If Dr. Lydgate had not been a medical man with specific views of medical research and progress the effect on his character of his marrying a flighty girl with no comprehension of his professional aims could not have been what it was; and so on.

Beginning with comparatively slight descriptions of men and man-

ners, such as are found in *Scenes of Clerical Life* (1858), George Eliot
soon proceeded to more complex kinds of fiction. *Adam Bede* (1859),
her first full-dress novel, has an element of pastoral idealism in the
character of the hero which recurs at intervals in George Eliot's work;
but it is significant that this note is connected with the dignity of work,
with the capacity to fit in usefully and happily to a social environment.
Superficially, the plot of *Adam Bede* might be considered melodramatic,
with its seduction of the pretty rustic maid by the squire and the subsequent excitement of infanticide and last-minute reprieve from the
gallows, but these violent elements take their place in the context of
the novel with an extraordinary quietness, deriving partly from the
author's sureness of psychological touch—the seducing squire, for
example is no villain of melodrama but a well-meaning if weak character
presented throughout with a sympathetic understanding—and partly
from her ability to anchor these events in the rhythm of daily life in the
countryside. The whole novel has the air of a postlapsarian pastoral—
no idealized story of shepherds and shepherdesses, but a story of virtue
and vice confronting each other in a society where in the last analysis
the dignity of labour and the simple virtues of faith and love can
redeem life from squalour into peace and orderliness. True, the idealistic
note is there, in the characters of Adam and Dinah, and the marriage
of these two at the end moves the story from the probable to the almost
purely symbolic; but there is sufficient earthiness in the novel as a
whole to remind us that we are not in the Garden of Eden, but in the
modern world, after the Fall.

The Mill on The Floss (1860) is a more complex novel, but again one
in which the moral problems of character are illustrated by the relation
between one character and another, those relations in turn growing
naturally out of the daily life and work of different members of a
community. There is an autobiographical impulse in this novel (Maggie
and Tom Tulliver are clearly projections in some degree of the young
Marian Evans and her brother) which further complicates its pattern,
giving it a pervasive emotion and sometimes an excessively high-pitched
note so that at moments it reads like the work of a passionate and gifted
adolescent. *Silas Marner* (1861) a simpler novel, much quieter in tone,
is little more than a symbolic fable, though a brilliantly executed one.
It has something of the tone of a fairy tale, with its story of the baby,
left at the door of the lonely weaver after his gold had been taken from
him, and the change in his character and way of life which his rearing
of the baby brings. This novel of redemption might be considered as
an antitype to Hawthorne's *Scarlet Letter*, the latter being the story of
the discovery of guilt and the former of the rediscovery of innocence.
Romola (1863) and *Felix Holt* (1866) are of less interest than *Middlemarch* (1871-2), George Eliot's masterpiece, where the exploration of
moral situations through the presentation of characters interacting on
each other and belonging to intersecting social groups is achieved with
a sustained brilliance. In a sense, the novel is one of moral discovery,

each of the more important characters learning the truth about himself or herself as a result of what happens to him (and of course what happens to him is never arbitrary, but the result of a combination of character and fortune). The resolution of the novel—where the beautiful and idealistic Dorothea marries, as her second husband, the sensitive but somewhat dimly defined Will Ladislaw—is perhaps the least satisfactory thing about it; it seems to indicate a purely symbolic picture of feminine idealism married to a combination of all the masculine virtues, namely sensitivity, understanding, and a zeal for public welfare. But this ending is the least important part of the novel, whose richness of texture belies the simplicity of its conclusion.

There is a delicacy of psychological perception in George Eliot's handling of Dorothea's marriage to Mr. Casaubon which is quite beyond anything Dickens was capable of in this manner. The way in which Casaubon's intellectual deficiencies are gradually developed and made symbolic of his physical and emotional deficiencies, with the implication that Dorothea's discovery of what Casaubon lacks as a man is part of her own discovery of herself as a woman, marks a new kind of subtlety and complexity in the Victorian novel, while to make Dorothea's and the reader's disillusionment with Casaubon produce in both a kind of sympathy with him is to show an awareness of some of the paradoxes of human relationships that gives a new dimension to prose fiction. Similarly, the marriage of Lydgate and Rosamond is presented with a fineness of understanding that transcends simple moral judgment, Rosamond's fundamental selfishness and naïve belief that other people exist primarily to satisfy her wants being shown not merely as a moral fault to be censored but as part of an essential childishness that has, in spite of everything, an appeal of its own, which is closely related to the reason why Lydgate married her in the first place.

There are other features of *Middlemarch* which contribute to making it one of the very greatest of English novels. The different characters and different contexts of living in town and country are shown intersecting in their interests and activities in a way which is fruitfully symbolic not only of the relationship between the individual and society, but also of one part of society with another. Country squire, clergyman, farmer, agricultural labourer, banker, doctor, workers and idlers in town and country, are shown in the complex network of interrelationships which itself is a microcosm of man in the world. The characters presented are thus more than individuals brought in as examples, illustrations, psychological types, or caricatures; they are both real and symbolic, both highly individual portraits and organic parts of a carefully organized plot. Fred Vincy, the well-meaning but weak young man, is a brilliantly shrewd study of a recognizable type; the last days of Mr. Featherstone are drawn with grim and vivid particularization; the downfall of Mr. Bulstrode—and especially the scene between his wife and him after she has heard of his disgrace—is done with a degree of truth and imaginative understanding that is positively astonishing;

and one could pick out other scenes and characters; but all these are elements in a grand design which weaves in and out of the novel and can be seen at last, when we view the novel as a whole from a certain distance, as paramount. The almost melodramatic apparatus George Eliot used to project certain important developments in the plot may strike the modern reader as somewhat forced, but it is not prominent enough to weaken the novel as a whole or to spoil the effect of life as it is lived, of provincial England at work, which is so important in the book.

Daniel Deronda (1876) contains some of George Eliot's most brilliant writing, but the novel seems to be conducted on two different levels of probability. As the story of Gwendolyn Harleth, the spoilt beauty who acquires moral character through suffering, the novel has psychological subtlety and moral power; but to find an adequate criterion on which the hollowness of Gwendolyn's world of empty social ambition is to be judged, George Eliot created Daniel Deronda, gentleman of mysterious birth who turns out to be the scion of a long line of Jewish sages and who eventually discovers it to be his destiny to reunite his ancient people in some new and unexplained way. Deronda is surrounded with dark figures of wisdom and beauty which make a strange (and deliberate) contrast to the social life of the fair English girls with their conventional families, and, mediating between the worlds of Semitic profundity and English conventionality, is the continental musician Klemser. One has the feeling that George Eliot is reaching out in this her last novel to something more profound and universal than any novel based on the merely English social scene could achieve. She does not quite achieve it because her different groups of characters move on different levels and as a result the moments when they come into contact with each other are not rendered convincingly (with the exception of the great scene where Klesmer, summoned to Gwendolyn who wants him to tell her how to be an actress, tries to open her eyes to the true nature of the world of art). But with all its defects, *Daniel Deronda* remains a remarkable novel, and one which seems to be straining to burst the limits of Victorian fiction.

It must be remembered that George Eliot was one of the Victorian 'sages' as well as a novelist, one of those who worried and thought and argued about religion, ethics, history, character, with all the concern felt by those most receptive to the many currents of new ideas flowing in on Victorian thought and most sensitive to their implications. A sage whose moral vision is most effectively communicated through realistic fiction is an unusual phenomenon—or, at least, was unusual at the time when George Eliot began to write. If it has become less unusual since, that is because George Eliot by her achievement in fiction permanently enlarged the scope of the novel. . . .

From *A Critical History of English Literature*, Secker & Warburg 1960, Vol. 4, pp. 1066–72.

ROBERT PREYER

Beyond the Liberal Imagination: Vision and Unreality in *Daniel Deronda*

There exists today a critical consensus as to the particular powers and shortcomings of George Eliot's novels. We admire her social insight, the masterful way in which she constructs and sets in motion a dense, particularized, and believable fictional world. This was the novelist who wrote, 'There is no private life which is not determined by a wider public life'.[1] Critics have been quoting this life ever since because no novelist, with the exception of Tolstoi, has conveyed the truth in that assertion in a more subtle, convincing, detailed, and realistic way. We admire as well her deep psychological observation, the careful, continual scrutiny of that area of experience which is most inaccessible to the trained student of society. Dr. Leavis has convincingly illustrated her mastery here, in the notation of 'inner life of impulse, the play of motive that issues in speech and act and underlies formed thought and conscious will.'[2] At a time when novelists tend to exploit either psychology or sociology to achieve their ends, her masterful combination of both sorts of interest seems astonishing and important. Where, we ask, are her successors? The question is probably unanswerable—but we can contribute something to it by investigating what went wrong in her last and most ambitious novel, *Daniel Deronda*. No one can fail to see that this work (which followed *Middlemarch*) is not satisfactory as a whole. Nowhere are her powers of psychological analysis and social observation exhibited in a happier light; yet they seem to be improperly used or related to a total intention which is hard to be clear about. Some new order of interest has obtruded itself and it is very irritating.

For a critic like Dr. Leavis there is no new order of interest. He finds instead 'a satisfaction from imaginative participation in exalted enthusiasms and self-devotions [that] would, if she could suddenly have gained the powers of analysis that in these regions she lacked, have surprised her'. (Leavis, p. 61). It amounts to an indulgence in daydreams; and wherever it occurs social and psychological realism go by the boards and an element of fairy-tale and fantasy sweep in. The seer

[1] *Felix Holt*, ch. III. All quotations from the novels are from the *Works of George Eliot*, Cabinet Ed., . . .

[2] F. R. Leavis, *The Great Tradition*, New York 1954, p. 128.

replaces the novelist; or as Leavis puts it, 'a magnificent intellect is worsted by emotional needs'.

In what follows I propose to take another look at this 'immaturity' and the reasons for its presence. It does not seem to me simply a matter of a writer being encouraged to abandon herself to sloppy feeling and thinking—and doing so. It is possible to argue that George Eliot was responding, in part at least, to an order of experience which fitted uneasily (if at all) into existing novelistic forms . . . George Eliot was attempting to extend and refine her account of the actual workings of sympathy and repulsion within the psyche. She had come to believe that the usual accounts of conduct, motivation, will, and aspiration needed to be enlarged and complicated; if they were not, man would increasingly acquiesce in the vision of himself as a being whose actions were determined by the operation of vast impersonal forces beyond his control. To remedy this situation she turned to the wisdom literature of the mystics and visionaries, emphasizing the way in which a receptivity to elective affinities and visions, to signs and portents, is related to the possibility of discovering a personal destiny and a socially useful vocation.

. . . Heroism, in an artist, consists in an openness to experience, a willingness to discard laboriously earned skills when they no longer apply. To be alive in this sense is always to risk the chance of losing the very tools by which one gains a livelihood . . . *Daniel Deronda* has something heroic about it. It offers a sustained and impressive account of an area of experience which had been largely ignored by Victorian intellectuals and, when treated by novelists, handled in a debased or fatuous way. The disaffections, the irrationality, the idealism, the sense of disconnection and loss, the yearning for a saving vocation—all these morbid symptoms are viewed seriously as responses appropriate to a grave distortion in the relations that obtained between the self and society. To have recognized interconnections between these vast subterranean movements of feeling, to articulate in novelistic terms the resulting restless discontent of spirit, was no mean achievement for a novelist. And to have related it to religion and developments in the conditions of work, to have taken it seriously as a portent of the future, was impressive indeed. George Eliot was responding to realities, as we know to our cost. And if today's realities seem as lurid and fevered as adolescent fantasies, we cannot blame George Eliot: her end as an artist, always, was verisimilitude.

. . . There is little or nothing of the 'Romantic Agony' in George Eliot's work. . . . The rationalist aspect of our author led her to a careful estimate of how large, impersonal environmental forces determine individual conduct. But along side this was a 'visionary' element which increasingly emphasized the way in which our receptivity (or lack of it) to signs and portents helps us to break free from the tyranny of habitual responses and to find out, in Lawrence's words, 'what the heart really wants after all'. This second aspect of her sensibility bulks very large in *Daniel Deronda*, which can be understood, perhaps, as an effort to convey the simultaneous workings of both aspects of reality.

One half of the book concerns the affairs of Gwendolen Harleth, a beautiful and wilful girl who commands the ability naturally to take precedence on social occasions. In common with other society figures, she shared 'a strong determination to have what was pleasant, with a total fearlessness in making themselves disagreeable or dangerous when they did not get it' She is formidable in the usual upper-class way; but she is also intelligent and in addition possesses a peculiarly personal charm. Those who feared her were also fond of her, intrigued 'by what may be called the iridescence of her character—the play of various, nay, contrary tendencies' (ch. IV). These contradictions are dramatically exemplified in a number of incidents that occur early in the book. We see her in moments when her will is of no avail and she is at the mercy of sudden and unexpected movements of impulse. The suddenly revealed picture of a dead face reduces her to hysterical fear; 'Solitude in any wide scene impressed her with an undefined feeling of immeasurable existence aloof from her, in the midst of which she was helplessly incapable of asserting herself.' These experiences naturally frightened her and, so far as possible, she repressed them, returning with relief to the normal social world where 'her will was of some avail'. We are shown that there was nothing in her environment to suggest that these moments of spiritual dread are anything other than morbid. 'This fountain of awe within her had not found its way into connection with the religion taught her or with any human relations' (ch. VI). The career of such a girl was bound to be problematic, or even tragic. 'So much pride and courage and sensitiveness and intelligence fixed in a destructive deadlock through false valuation and self-ignorance—this', writes Dr. Leavis, 'is what makes Gwendolen a tragic figure' (p. 136). She is unable to comprehend the 'morbid' promptings of her consciousness and too sensitive to smother them.

Her problems are nudged into consciousness by a series of accidental meetings with a mysterious Daniel Deronda. She feels, for the first time, that she is being judged, not judging, and that this insufferable young man lives by a standard of excellence which she does not comprehend. A second shock occurs when her natural musical superiority is not admitted by competent judges. Once again, there is the painful recognition that a higher standard of excellence exists and is meaningful to certain people. The point is made in a number of encounters. One side of her nature tells her than no one would look twice at Miss Arrowpoint if it were not for her money and social position. But the side of her nature which was later to be sensitized by Deronda admitted 'a certain mental superiority which could not be explained away—an exasperating thoroughness in her musical accomplishment, a fastidious discrimination in her general tastes, which made it impossible to force her admiration and kept you in awe of her standard' (ch. VI). There were elements in Gwendolen's nature which responded deeply to the intellectual and moral possibilities of which she was now becoming conscious, and there were elements which feared them. 'This subjection to a possible self, a self not to be absolutely predicted about, caused her some astonishment and terror: her favourite key of life—doing as she liked—seemed to fail her, and she could not foresee what at a given moment she might like to do' (ch. XIII).

It was at this moment that financial catastrophe overwhelmed her family and a 'suitable' marriage seemed the only possible solution. Her newly awakened instincts warned her that Grandcourt was formidable and deadly, that he induced 'a lotus-eater's stupor', that he was 'a handsome lizard of some hitherto unknown species, not of the lively, darting kind'. She has received warnings about his devious past. But at the moment of crisis, she is unable to break the old slavery to egotistic satisfactions; her decision is dictated by the social forces about her. A set of rationalizations quickly cover up the struggle: she is doing this for her mother. Grandcourt's 'absence of demonstrativeness' is not sinister, it merely implies that he will be easily managed; a disreputable past seemed impossibly remote from the 'Mr. Grandcourt who had come to Diplow in order apparently to make a chief epoch in her destiny' (ch. XIII). Her egotism required that he be seen in this light—as a convenience she freely chose—and with this lie she opened a path into a lifetime of wretchedness. For Grandcourt was all ego—nothing can mar his exquisite contempt for others, no scruples hamper his will to command.

This half of the book, of course, has been highly praised. It offers a detailed examination of the way in which a failure to heed our deepest awareness brings nemesis in its train. As such, it constitutes what we might call a negative demonstration of the thesis George Eliot wishes to propound. The positive side of the thesis, the account of a man who follows his deepest awareness and achieves Salvation, has been damned by nearly all critics. It centres on Daniel Deronda, a youth who has little egotism and a large supply of those 'natural sympathies' which Gwendolen so longed to possess. Because of these advantages we are asked to judge him by a higher standard than applies to Gwendolen. His temptation is not worldliness but spiritual sloth, an unwillingness resolutely to seek out and risk a course of action that is consonant with his nature. As a young man 'he longed to have a sort of apprenticeship to life which would not shape him too definitely and rob him of the choice that might come from a free growth'. He errs on the side of 'reflective hesitation', 'questioning whether it were worth while to take part in the battle of the world: [a common mood for] young men in whom the unproductive labour of questioning is sustained by three or five per cent on capital' (chs XVI, XVII). What forces him out of this mood is a 'natural sympathy' first with Meyrick and then with Mirah. He sees that 'A too reflective and diffusive sympathy was in danger of paralysing in him that indignation against wrong and that selectness of fellowship which are the conditions of moral force' (ch. XXXII), and so looks about for some external event or inward light which would urge him into a

definite course of action, compress his will. To his dismay, he finds what
he seeks in Mordecai, a penniless Jewish visionary. Here we come again
to the theme of elective affinities, 'that mutual influence of dissimilar
destinies' which so intrigued George Eliot. Deronda had gone to
Mordecai for a particular piece of information: if he got the information
he wanted, he wouldn't go further and ask why Mordecai seemed to have
some expectation from him which was disappointed. At this point, he
experienced, as was wont with him, a quick change of mental light,
shifting his point of view to that of the person whom he had been thinking
of hitherto chiefly as serviceable to his own purposes. . . . 'It might be
that he had neared and parted as one can imagine two ships doing, each
freighted with an exile who would have recognized the other if the two
could have looked out face to face. Not that there is any likelihood of a
peculiar tie between me and this poor fellow. . . . But I wonder whether
there is much of that momentous mutual missing between people who
interchange blank looks, or even long for one another's absence in a
crowded place' (ch. XI).

Mordecai insists that Deronda has a mission, that he was put on
earth to fulfil the dreams and aspirations of the Jewish people. Deronda
must choose—either he accepts or rejects this proposition. On the face
of it, it is absurd. Deronda sensibly considers the possibility that his
friend's visionary excitement may have turned his wishes into an over-
mastering impression, causing him to read a series of accidental meetings
as a divine fulfilment. 'Was such a temper of mind,' he asks himself,
'likely to accompany that wise estimate of consequences which is the
only safeguard from fatal error, even to ennobling motive?' The logical
answer was no—but Deronda takes more into account than logic.
There may be cases where 'a wise estimate of consequences is fused in
the fires of that passionate belief which determines the consequences it
believes in. The inspirations of the world have come in that way too:
even strictly measuring science could hardly have got on without that
forecasting ardour which feels the agitations of discovery beforehand,
and has a faith in its preconception that surmounts many failures of
experiment. And in relation to human motives and actions, passionate
belief has a fuller efficacy. Here enthusiasm may have the validity of
proof, and, happening in one soul, give the type of what will one day be
general.' Mordecai may be a sort of saving mutation or spirit: 'No
formulas for thinking will save us mortals from mistake in our imperfect
apprehension of the matter to be thought about . . . perhaps an emotional
intellect may have absorbed into its passionate vision of possibilities
some truth of what will be—the more comprehensive massive life
feeding theory with new material, as the sensibility of the artist seizes
combinations which science [later] explains and justifies' (ch. XLI).

Deronda is persuaded of this—perhaps he is the only one who is—and
goes off on his nebulous mission. Before parting, he explains it all to
Gwendolen, and as a by-product of this meeting, she finally comes to
see what her own problem has always been: 'she was for the first time

feeling the pressure of a vast mysterious movement, for the first time being dislodged from her supremacy in her own world . . . all the troubles of her widowhood and wifehood had still left her with the implicit impression which had accompanied her since childhood, that whatever surrounded her was somehow specially for her' (ch. XLIII). She now feels a shock greater than jealousy; she feels humiliation, an awareness of the continuous egotism which has blocked her access into a wider and freer realm of being. She is now ready to join those others who are fore-runners of the new dispensation.

Here then, is George Eliot's final account of the way in which sympathy or the lack of it, egotism, operate to effect our destinies. The burden of her work had emphasized the ways in which men were con-ditioned and determined; here was an effort to redress the balance. We may look upon it, to borrow a phrase from Professor Trilling, as an effort 'to make us aware of the particularity of selves, and the high authority of the self in its quarrel with its society and its culture.'[3] The task seemed urgent enough and was undertaken, one might almost say, as a duty.[4]

Her failure to be convincing in that part of the work given over to Daniel Deronda cannot be explained on the grounds that she had outgrown her genius—after all, the Gwendolen Harleth aspect of the book has received the highest critical acclaim. The failure, if we accept it as that, may lie in the method of presentation or in the difficulty of handling ideas of this sort in works of realistic fiction. It may be that any convincing account of a hidden or non-perceptual base to human experience requires some other genre for its presentation—the romance or dream vision forms might be suggested. In works of this sort, ele-ments of fairy tale, of psychomachia, and of the traditional quest theme are accepted as a matter of course. In this case a critic could argue that the failure to satisfy the normal expectations of novel readers constitutes the basic flaw. (Poets and romance writers are licensed to handle varieties of experience which violate conventions of verisimilitude that hold for novelists. A novelist makes one sort of contract with the reader, a poet or romancer another, and violations are punishable in any critical court.) This line of reasoning ignores the fact that George Eliot (and most great writers) commit themselves only to the vaguest of contracts (in this case, to the proposition that 'art is the nearest thing to life . . . of a mode of amplifying experience and extending our contact with our fellow-men beyond the bounds of our personal lot'). She was entitled to ignore the conventions agreed upon by the bulk of her middle-class readers if they got in her way. After all, a writer of fiction is traditionally entitled to deal in what might have been, what may be, or even what is not.

[3] Lionel Trilling, *Freud and the Crisis of Our Culture*, Boston 1955, p. 33.
[4] In 'Leaves From a Notebook' she gives, as marks of a serious writer, an ability to 'animate long known and neglected truths' and to make, 'by a wise emphasis here, and a wise disregard there. . . . [a] more useful or beautiful proportion to aims or motives', *Essays*, pp. 362-3.

A second critical approach might ignore the genre argument, pointing instead to the need for a more evocative, even distorted, language if an author is to convince us of the reality of little known modes of being. Dr. Leavis seems to take this tack when he contrasts her 'ethical' vision with Lawrence's 'religious' awareness, basing his distinction on stylistic grounds.[5] The danger here has been indicated by Winters and others, namely, that it does no sort of justice to the *ideas* of a writer. It is an important controversy but I will not get into it at this point.

Instead, I want to close by pointing to the limitations of a narrowly literary concern with the 'success' or 'failure' of individual works of art. Such a concern does not do justice to the *interest* of a literary work of any magnitude; for that interest may have wide ramifications in a number of directions. Thus, it is commonly held that the novel was a principal means of spreading and refining the ethos of the middle class, its hopes and aspirations, its sense of reality. . . . George Eliot and many others . . . were aware that the heart was going out of that ethos, that it no longer persuaded to action. It is significant that they related this failure in liberal, humane culture to the earlier failure in the powers of conviction which religious ideas exercised. The 'culture' of Eliot and Arnold had its roots in those ideas: their language of sympathy and fellow-feeling, of sweetness and light, had been designed to replace the anachronistic language of theology. George Eliot, especially, was looking for some way of rejuvenating the attitude of mind which supplied conviction and dynamism to the holder of these beliefs. She was not prepared, as was Pater's Marius, to settle back in a supine and passive aesthetic admiration of an attitude which had lost all contact with social actualities: 'Revelation, vision, the *seeing* of a perfect humanity, in a perfect world, he had always set that above the *having*, or even the *doing*, of anything. For such vision, if received with due attitude on his part, was, in reality, the *being* something, and such was surely a pleasant offering or sacrifice to whatever gods might be, observant of him.'[6] These are the terms in which the interest of *Daniel Deronda* comes clear. It was a response to this liberal failure, a last effort to break new ground in an effort to persuade readers of the need for moral awareness and the significance of individual endeavour for the general good. The earlier liberal cry of freedom from external domination, *laissez-faire*, had become a mockery; and with the triumph of 'the historical method' ethical values seemed increasingly irrelevant to the field of social dynamics and power politics. Ideas and ways of behaviour were seen as historically conditioned and transient. Even science, with its magnificent technical equipment and its record of achievement, could offer no particular goals outside its own field. The area of determinism in human life seemed to expand every generation. Given this situation George Eliot was driven to the effort we have indicated, an effort to expand the area of human freedom by breaking through the

[5] F. R. Leavis, *D. H. Lawrence, Novelist*, London 1955, pp. 110-12.
[6] Walter Pater, *Marius the Epicurean* (London, 1896) p. 346.

usual accounts of the way we are psychologically determined. It seems to me that her pioneering steps in this direction have never received a due attention.

From *Victorian Studies*, Vol. 4, September 1960, pp. 33–54, (33–5, 48–54).

FRED C. THOMSON

Felix Holt as Classic Tragedy

The unpopularity of *Felix Holt, the Radical* has usually, and with some justice, been attributed to the intricate legal plot, the uncongenial political background, and the dramatic deficiency of Felix as an apostle of social reform. Praise of the novel has been limited mainly to those portions involving Mrs Transome and her son Harold, the progeny of an adulterous affair with the family lawyer Jermyn. What has never received sufficient attention is that the characterization and story of Mrs Transome and Harold (as distinct from the rather stiffly abrasive romance of Felix and Esther Lyon) are no less experimental than the law and politics, and perhaps more successful in execution.

There seems good reason to believe that the political material was not a part of George Eliot's original design and was introduced some time after she had started the novel.[1] A little over a month before she recorded in her journal having 'begun' what was to be *Felix Holt*,[2] she had been at work on the first version of her blank verse tragedy *The Spanish Gipsy*. On February 21, 1865, she was into the fourth act when George Henry Lewes took the MS away from her, 'precisely because it was in that stage of Creation or "Werden", in which the idea of the characters predominates over the incarnation'.[3] That her interest in tragedy, especially the Greek, continued during the following months is indicated by her reading list for May 10: 'Aeschylus, Theatre of the Greeks, Klein's Hist. of the Drama, etc.' (Journal). And on June 15

---

[1] Discussed in my article 'The Genesis of *Felix Holt*,' *PMLA* LXXIV, Dec. 1959, 576–84.

[2] March 29 1865. See MS Journal, 1861–77, Tinker Collection, Yale University Library.

[3] Gordon S. Haight (ed.), *The George Eliot Letters*, New Haven, 1954–1955, Vol. 4, 301.

she noted, 'Read again Aristotle's Poetics, with fresh admiration.' On the whole, evidence suggests that she meant *Felix Holt* to conform in some way to the example of Greek drama.[4] Frederic Harrison, as he read the MS of Volume 1, was moved to write 'I feel even at this moment as if I had been present and seen some great tragedy and cannot shake off the impression that I have lately *witnessed* something terrible.'[5] And in the completed work he was sensitive to a special timbre.

'I found myself taking it up as I take up Tennyson or Shelley or Browning and thinking out the sequences of thoughts suggested by the undertones of the thought and the harmony of the lines. Can it be right to put the subtle finish of a poem into the language of a prose narrative?'[6]

This may sound a bit extravagant, but Harrison was right in discerning that at least in the Transome history George Eliot was exploring 'a really new species of literature . . . a romance constructed in the artistic spirit and aim of a poem,'[7] more specifically a tragedy after the classic model.

In her 'Notes on the Spanish Gipsy and Tragedy in General,' George Eliot defines tragedy thus:

'Suppose for a moment that our conduct at great epochs was determined entirely by reflection, without the intermediate intervention of feeling which supersedes reflection, our determination as to the right would consist in an adjustment of our individual needs to the dire necessities of our lot, partly as to our natural constitution, partly as sharers of life with our fellow-beings. Tragedy consists in the terrible difficulty of this adjustment—

"The dire strife of poor Humanity's afflicted will,
Struggling in vain with ruthless destiny."

. . . a good tragic subject must represent a possible, sufficiently probable, not a common action: and to be really tragic, it must represent irreparable collision between the individual and the

---

[4] There is an allusion to the doctrine of catharsis in a passage at the end of the introduction: 'For there is seldom any wrong-doing which does not carry along with it some downfall of blindly climbing hopes, some hard entail of suffering . . . such as has raised the pity and terror of men ever since they began to discern between will and destiny.' See also George Eliot's letter to Frederic Harrison on August 15 1866: 'And again, it is my way, (rather too much so perhaps) to . . . urge the human sanctities through tragedy through pity and terror as well as admiration and delights,' GE *Letters* IV, 301. The novel also contains such stock devices of Greek tragedy as the 'recognition' scene (ch. xlvii). Harold Transome, it may be added, fits quite nicely Aristotle's definition of the tragic hero, a man 'not pre-eminently virtuous and just, whose misfortune, however, is brought upon him not by vice and depravity but by some error of judgment of the number of those in the enjoyment of great reputation and prosperity', *The Works of Aristotle*, trans. W. D. Ross [Oxford 1924] Vol. 11.

[5] GE *Letters*, IV 220.

[6] Harrison, *op cit.*, pp. 284–5.

[7] *Ibid.*

general (in differing degrees of generality). It is the individual with whom we sympathize, and the general of which we recognize the irresistible power. The truth of this test will be seen by applying it to the greatest tragedies. The collision of Greek tragedy is often that between hereditary, entailed Nemesis and the peculiar individual lot, awakening our sympathy, of the particular man or woman whom the Nemesis is shown to grasp with terrific force. . . . A tragedy has not to expound why the individual must give way to the general; it has to show that it is compelled to give—the tragedy consisting in the struggle involved and often in the entirely calamitous issue in spite of a grand submission.'[8]

The Transome story qualifies as a 'good tragic subject', being the representation of a 'possible, sufficiently probable, not a common action'. The mysterious and sensational ingredients remove it safely from the commonplace; yet there is nothing in the plot that could be deemed impossible. The worst improbability is that all the persons necessary to the unravelling of the plot should be assembled at once in Treby; and this has a philosophical justification in George Eliot's concept of 'that mutual influence of dissimilar destinies' (ch. III).[9] Coincidence held for her none of the attractions of operational expedience that Dickens and Trollope exploited. She always used it sparingly.

In Felix Holt there is conspicuously the 'irreparable collision between the individual and the general' requisite for a 'really tragic' subject. Mrs Transome has collided with the general moral law, and she must suffer for it ever after. Her passively remorseful submissiveness to the consequences of her transgression cannot prevent catastrophe. Harold's collision with the general is of a more complex sort. He is, in the first place, a victim of his mother's sin, helpless to stave off eventual disgrace. But like Oedipus he is also the ironic hastener of Nemesis. An intractable egoist, complacent about the justness of his conduct, he shrugs off his mother's plea for leniency towards Jermyn, not knowing what hard wall of preordained conditions he is rushing against. Mrs Transome feels the shock now, as Harold will later.

'I will arrange nothing amicably with him' said Harold decisively. 'If he has ever done anything scandalous as our agent, let him bear the infamy. And the right way to throw the infamy on him is to show the world that he has robbed us, and that I mean to punish him. Why do you wish to shield such a fellow, mother? It has been chiefly through him that you have had to lead such a thrifty miserable life— you who used to make as brilliant a figure as a woman need wish.'

[8] John W. Cross (ed.) George Eliot's Life as Related in her Letters and Journals 3 vols, Edinburgh and London, 1885, 3, 41–9. Although the 'Notes' probably postdate the completed Spanish Gipsy in 1868, there is no reason to suppose that George Eliot's views on tragedy had been materially revised since 1864–65.
[9] Quotations are from the 1st edition of Felix Holt, 3 vols, 1866.

Mrs Transome's rising temper was turned into a horrible sensation, as painful as a sudden concussion from something hard and immovable when we have struck out with our fist, intending to hit something warm, soft, and breathing, like ourselves. Poor Mrs Transome's strokes were sent jarring back on her by a hard unalterable past. She did not speak in answer to Harold, but rose from the chair as if she gave up the debate (ch. XXXVI).'

Harold has still to learn that destiny is 'laid upon us by the acts of other men as well as our own.' (ch. XLIX).

Esther, too, when she becomes involved with the Transome destinies, is confronted by the general. She must choose between the silken idleness at Transome Court and an austere life of service and toil with Felix. Since Felix is obviously intended to be a nobler person than Harold, her vacillations may seem a trifle academic: yet to George Eliot the struggle was by no means academic. Her heroines have dangerous penchants for second-raters. Witness Maggie and Stephen, Romola and Tito, Dorothea and Casaubon (and afterwards Will). The choice which seems so clear may well have given Esther pause.[10] Like the heroines above, she was fundamentally at war not with the alternatives of luxury and hardship, but with her dependence, her need for someone to 'lean upon'. With Felix in prison, his pardon still in doubt, and his aversion to marriage still not definitely overcome, Esther dreads finding herself alone and in circumstances repugnant to her fastidious sensibilities. Harold and Transome Court could at least rescue her from material insecurity. 'And there is a pernicious falsity in the pretence that a woman's love lies above the range of such temptations' (ch. XLIII). Her final decision comes when she realises that they could not give her the essential spiritual security.

The controlling theme of 'hereditary, entailed Nemesis' that collides with the 'peculiar individual lot,' is best expressed in the motto for ch. XLVIII:

'Tis law steadfast as the throne of Zeus—
Our days are heritors of days gone by'.
                    Aeschylus, *Agamemnon*

In *Felix Holt*, however, Nemesis is converted from the utterly implacable Greek concept to a rather positivistic form—a severe but ultimately compassionate moral determinism, whereby deeds make an indissoluble unity of past, present, and future; but whereby the regenerative power of human sympathy has room to mitigate the grievous consequences of moral errors. The emphasis in the denouncement is on pity, for Mrs Transome as well as for Harold. If Mrs Transome's sin has brought inevitable misfortune to herself and Harold, Harold is not to be exempted from having pity on 'the heart

[10] 'That changing face was the perfect symbol of her mixed susceptible nature, in which battle was inevitable, and the side of victory uncertain' (ch. XXXVII).

that loved him'. That he does so, at Ether's tactful instigation, resolves the tragedy on a properly affirmative note. 'The art which leaves the soul in despair is laming to the soul, and is denounced by the healthy sentiment of active community.'[11]

It should now be fairly evident that in *Felix Holt* George Eliot was adhering to the principles set forth in the 'Notes on the Spanish Gipsy and Tragedy in General'. The problem remains to explain why so many readers have felt disappointment in the results of her experiment. To begin with, the Transome story is too much diluted by the politics and law, and is almost lost sight of through long stretches of the novel while George Eliot focuses on the election campaign and the problems of Felix and Esther—problems that until the discovery of Esther's identity in ch. XXXVI barely impinge upon those of Harold and his mother. Mrs Transome, who virtually dominates the opening chapters, disappears from the scene towards the end of Volume I, not to reappear until Volume III. Harold enters only briefly in Volume II, and then in a strictly political role. Moreover, there are one or two features (suggestive of classic tragedy) that distinguish *Felix Holt* from George Eliot's previous 'English' stories and show her working on ground relatively alien to her genius.

First of all, one notices the generally higher social plane of the action and protagonists. Mrs Transome, with her gloomy eloquence and regal bearing, is a type quite new in George Eliot's fiction, one envisioned, it would seem, to meet the requirements of a tragic heroine in the grand tradition.

> She had that high-born imperious air which would have marked her as an object of hatred and reviling by a revolutionary mob. Her person was too typical of social distinctions to be passed by with indifference by any one: it would have fitted an empress in her own right, who had had to rule in spite of faction, to dare the violation of treaies and dread retributive invasions, to grasp after new territories to be defiant in desperate circumstances, and to feel a woman's hunger of the heart for ever unsatisfied(ch. I).

A passage deleted from the MS of chapter I reads:

> If any one had wanted to paint an imaginary portrait of such a worn, eager, desolate-hearted empress, he might have found a good model in this velvet-clad, grey-haired woman on the background of the broad staircase with its massive balustrade, worn matting and patches of dark red carpet.[12]

Mrs Transome is 'wont to look queenly of an evening' in her mended garments. To her servant Denner she is a sort of 'goddess' whose

[11] Cross, *op. cit.*, III, 49.
[12] I, fols 42–43. The MS is in the British Museum. The present study is based on microfilms.

'rhetoric and temper belonged to her superior rank, her grand person and her piercing black eyes' (ch. XXXIX). Elsewhere she is described as a 'Hecuba-like woman' (ch. XXXIX).[13] . . .

Another way in which *Felix Holt* is distinguishable from its predecessors is the relative compactness of the time scheme, a major feature of classic tragedy. Of all George Eliot's novels, the action of this transpires within the shortest period. Between Harold's arrival at Transome Court on September 1, 1832, and the wedding of Felix and Esther the following May, only nine months elapse: and the crucial events of the story, capped by Esther's flight from Transome Court in ch. I, occur within only seven months, from September to March. This effort to achieve a greater dramatic unity of time was not altogether fortunate in its results. For one thing, the compressed time span forbade the patient cumulative evolvement of characters that had given the *Mill on the Floss* so much of its force. George Eliot usually did best when she had several years at her disposal, during which she could bring out patiently and through myriads of little incidents the idiosyncrasies of her people. Here she had to distil the data of long observation into set passages of descriptive characterizations, like those of Mrs Transome (ch. I) of Harold (ch. VIII), or of Denner (ch. I).

Although many scenes in *Felix Holt* are in dialogue form, less can be learned about the characters from what they say than from what George Eliot tells us directly. With the striking exceptions of chs. I and II, the conversation is singularly non-dimensional, serving to advance the plot more than the characterizations. . . .

In *Felix Holt*, as often in the Greek drama, the plot and outcome of the action hinge upon events outside the boundaries of the story itself. This antecedent history is available to any reader alert to the scattered clues and able to arrange them in a chronological pattern. Sometimes the information is directly narrated, like the tale of Esther's parentage (ch. VI); sometimes, as in the case of Mrs Transome's guilt, it is more obliquely presented. It is possible to date, to the year, most of the important occurrences prior to 1832, when the novel opens.[14] Even so, several very important keys to an understanding of the story, such as

---

[13] On March 25 1864 George Eliot was 'reading the sorrows of the aged Hecuba with great enjoyment. I wish an immortal could be got out of *my* sorrows, that people might be the better for them two thousand years hence', GE *Letters*, IV, 139.

[14] A similar schedule can be worked out, almost to the day, for events within the temporal frame of the action—at least well into Volume II. After ch. XXIV, and increasingly in Vol. III, adherence to a strict time scheme becomes less careful. Clues to specific dates are rare, usually only the month being indicated. As she approached her conclusion, George Eliot seemed to relax from the arduousness of plotting. By ch. XXXIX the legal mysteries have all been cleared away and there is space to study Esther's adjustments to her new circumstances. Once again George Eliot is in congenial territory, with divided desires in her heroine and a moral dilemma to work upon. The salient events are more widely dispersed and not so firmly linked in a day-to-day sequence.

the motivation of Felix and the circumstances of Mrs Transome's liaison with Jermyn, are left vague and undeveloped.

This making everything depend so heavily on what took place before the opening of the book was an innovation for George Eliot; it was not done to nearly the same extent in *Adam Bede*, *The Mill on the Floss*, *Silas Marner* or *Romola*. But in order to stay within the self-imposed time limits, George Eliot seems throughout to be obeying what might be called a narrative impulse. Hitherto the broader temporal latitude of the novels had permitted the plot to unfold leisurely. It had to wait while the character ripened. In *Felix Holt* the characters have to keep pace with the story as best as they can. There is much that must happen, and the time is short. How strong this narrative impulse was can be judged by comparing the factually informative interview of Jermyn and Christian in ch. XXI with the psychologically revealing meeting of Bulstrode and Raffles in ch. LIII of *Middlemarch*.

If George Eliot was deliberately trying to adapt the functions and techniques of Greek drama to her novel, it must be conceded that she fell short of her aim. The total impression left by *Felix Holt* is rather of Elizabethan luxuriance, with an injection too, one fears, of grand opera.[15] The indictments of superfluity and diffusion of interest cannot be refuted, and the machinery of the plot does sometimes need oiling. In *Middlemarch*, George Eliot returned to the type of tragedy she had always understood so well and could give its proper form—the obscure and blundering lives of those

> who found for themselves no epic life wherein there was a constant unfolding of far-resonant action; perhaps only a life of mistakes, the offspring of a certain spiritual grandeur ill-matched with the meanness of opportunity; perhaps a tragic failure which found no sacred poet and sank unswept into oblivion.[16]

But as an experiment in expanding the horizons of prose fiction, *Felix Holt* deserves more commendation than it has received. To re-examine the Transome plot in the context of classic tragedy results in a far more satisfactory concept of what the novel is really about than the Victorian reviewers reached. The prominent plot, the themes of Nemesis and the collision of the individual with the general, the tragically moulded

[15] George Eliot evidently had a taste for the sometimes banal dramatic values in opera. In July 1863, she wrote Sara Hennell, 'Rigoletto is unpleasant but it is superlatively fine tragedy in the nemesis—I think I don't know a finer', GE *Letters*, IV, 92–3. On June 13 1864, she heard Cherubini's *Medea*; and on July 3 *Faust* which thrilled her 'by the great symbolical situations and by the music' (Journal). She was also reading Shakespeare during the germinal months of *Felix Holt*.

[16] Prelude to *Middlemarch*, Riverside Edition, Boston, 1956, p. 3. Cf. George Eliot's letter to John Blackwood on July 9 1860, describing Maggie Tulliver as 'a character essentially noble but liable to great error—error that is anguish to its own nobleness . . .', GE *Letters*, III, 318.

characters, the heightened rhetoric, the compressed line span, the elaborate underpinning of antecedent history all point to a source of influence that should not be neglected in any effort to interpret the book.

From *Nineteenth-Century Fiction*, Vol. 16, 1961, pp. 47–58 (47–52, 54, 56–8).

IAN GREGOR

The Two Worlds of *Adam Bede*

> One begins to suspect at length that there is no direct connection
> between eyelashes and morals . . .
>
> *Adam Bede* (ch. xv)

'My new story haunts me a good deal', George Eliot wrote to her publisher in October 1857, 'and I shall start it without delay. It will be a country story—full of the breath of cows and the scent of hay'. This is the first description we have of *Adam Bede*, and in the century that divides us from the publication of that novel it has been echoed, in different tones of voice, many times. In the 1870's we find Henry James remarking that 'in *Adam Bede* the quality seems gilded by a sort of autumn haze, an afternoon light, of meditation', and recently Dr Leavis observed that its success is conditioned by its 'charm'. If, however, there have been many voices to repeat that *Adam Bede* is a 'country story' there have been others, hardly less numerous, to remind us that it is very much a novel by the author of *Middlemarch*, a novel animated by a serious moral purpose. In recent years a number of critics, anxious to rescue *Adam Bede* from what they feel to be patronizing acclaim, have sought to stress this aspect of the novel, either by relating it to the whole convention of serious pastoral, or by seeing it as a direct exploration of the basis of the right conduct. . . .[1]

. . . Time for all its meticulous appearance in this novel is not 'our' time. In spite of the repeated references to days, and dates, and months, the page of this calendar never really turns. The time may be 1799, but George Eliot is writing *Adam Bede* from a memory of a memory, and 1799 is 'a point in the past', near enough to avoid the remoteness of

---

[1] See note at the end of the passage.

'history', far enough away to escape 'the present'. It is historically dated in much the same way as western films are dated '1870', and traditional public school stories '1910'. We hear of the Napoleonic wars, but the rumble is a distant one, and 'the turn of the century' in *Adam Bede* is an archetypal 'turn'. The seasons mirror the narrative. In high summer we have Arthur's Coming-of-Age party and the climax of his passion for Hetty. As the year moves towards autumn and winter we have their exposure by Adam, Arthur's departure, and, in November, Adam's betrothal to Hetty:

> It has nothing to her—putting her arm through Adam's; but she knew he cared a good deal about her arm through his and she wished to care. Her heart beat no faster and she looked at the half-bare hedgerows and the ploughed field with the same sense of oppressive dullness as before.

The hedgerows finally became bare, Hetty's misery deepens and in February, to conceal her shame, she leaves Hayslope to search for Arthur. And we have the miserable journeys, through the bleak and cold countryside, under leaden skies which become dark in the late afternoon. March comes and the very day that Hetty and Adam were to have been married is the date fixed for her execution. But better times return. Adam and Dinah are married after the harvest festival and Mr Irwine makes the conjunction explicit, 'what better harvest from that painful seedtime could there be than this?'[2]

. . . 'A story of the country, with the breath of cows and the scent of hay . . .'; George Eliot might describe *Adam Bede* in this way, but it is also a novel which leads towards a statement about the function of tragedy in classical terms: '. . . It is not ignoble to feel that the fuller life which a sad experience has brought is worth our own personal share of pain . . . The growth of higher feeling within us is like the growth of a faculty, bringing with it a sense of added strength; we can no more wish to return to a narrower sympathy, than a painter or musician can wish to return to his cruder manner, or a philosopher to his less complete formula.' In this passage we come close not only to a central statement about the moral tragedy of this particular novel, but to a statement of George Eliot's attitude to fiction in general. How close can be judged by comparing it with this extract from one of her reviews:

> The greatest benefit we owe to the artist, whether painter, poet or novelist is the extension of our sympathies. Appeals founded on generalisations and statistics require sympathy ready-made, a moral sentiment already in activity; but a picture of human life, such as a

___

[2] The function of time in *Adam Bede* has frequently been noted by critics of the novel, particularly Dorothy Van Ghent and Maurice Hussey. To see, however, the full complexities of this, it is worth looking at W. J. Harvey, 'The Treatment of Time in Adam Bede', *Anglia*, Autumn 1957. That the time scheme is sometimes inaccurate is indicated by Daniel P. Deneau, 'Inconsistencies and Inaccuracies in Adam Bede', *Nineteenth-Century Fiction*, June 1959.

great artist can give, surprises even the trivial and the selfish into that attention to what is apart from themselves, which may be called the raw material of moral sentiment.

What the reader has to learn from fiction generally has, in *Adam Bede* to be learnt by the characters themselves. In various ways, and with varying degrees of emphasis, four characters gradually come to learn the truth about themselves, to learn their essential vanity, and in consequence to give 'attention to what is apart from themselves' . . . In *Adam Bede*, Mr V. S. Pritchett writes 'we are shocked by two things: the treatment of Hetty Sorrel and the marriage of Dinah and Adam at the end.'[3] He elaborates this by saying that, in the case of Hetty, George Eliot was working out a personal fantasy, and that, in the case of Dinah and Adam, she refused to face the nature of sexual passion. In isolating these faults I suggest that Mr Pritchett is pin-pointing exactly the places where the two worlds of the novel touch, but fail to intersect.

We do not need to indulge in psychological speculation to discover why the final treatment of Hetty is unsatisfying. She is an inhabitant of the pastoral world who has strayed into the world of moral enquiry and tragic destiny. Hetty lives simply by the coercive morality of the community and, when this is broken, she is destroyed; she has no life apart from this. — *Real life?*

If . . . we decide to put . . . questions about innocence and guilt and justice aside, and see Hetty as a conventional victim in a folk tale, then immediately the other characters look distorted and unsatisfactory. And this brings us to Mr. Pritchett's second objection to *Adam Bede*, the marriage of Adam and Dinah. Here again George Eliot has crossed the line between a conventional and a representational art. Unlike Hetty, Adam is a man we *are* called upon to understand in depth; where she is static and bewildered, he is evolving and aware. And the condition of this evolution is that he has to face experiences which bite deeply into him, modifying and altering his attitudes—his father's death—Hetty's desertion and her conviction. As Mrs Barbara Hardy remarks, 'at the beginning Adam has as much to learn as Lear'[4] There may be disagreement about the scale of this emphasis but there can be no doubt that the emphasis itself is correct. When Adam remarks to Arthur: 'I don't see how the thing's to be made any other than hard. There's a sort of damage, sir, that can't be made up for,' we feel that this is the fruit of a better lesson, which he has learnt with pain and difficulty. It has tragic *weight* behind it. Unlike Hetty's, Adam's career cannot be assumed into gesture and mime, it must have a representational reality about it. The marriage to Dinah runs counter to this. Individuality and complexity suddenly become ironed out; our attention is no longer directed towards Adam and Dinah but to 'the bond of marriage', signalizing that the broken community has been made whole again. The

Adam changes

3 *The Living Novel*, pp. 83–4.
4 *The Novels of George Eliot*, p. 37.

sexual element is omitted, not, as Mr Pritchett suggests, at the dictates of Victorian taste, but because George Eliot has altered her fictional style from moral realism to pseudo-pastoral. Everything in the closing chapters of the novel is designed to accomplish this, the careful placing of the Harvest Supper before the wedding, the stylized meeting on a high hill, surrounded 'by the still lights and shadows and the great embracing sky'. A tableau ending has been given to a novel which, for much of its length, has been concerned with the rejection of appearances. The objection is not to the marriage of Adam and Dinah, but to the facility of its realization. To invoke the 'pastoral pattern' is simply to reduce in status the moral drama which the novel has been concerned to describe. Marriage may fittingly conclude the pattern, but not the marriage of two people who have been presented in the realistic way that Dinah and Adam have, a way calculatedly endorsing George Eliot's earlier irony—'let all people who hold unexceptionable opinions act unexceptionably.' The marriage neutralizes the irony.

Both the things that shock us in *Adam Bede*, the treatment of Hetty and the marriage of Adam and Dinah, proceed from the common defect that George Eliot is extremely uncertain about the *kind* of novel she is writing. She describes the situation and she resolves its conflict by an appeal to a pastoral art; she develops the situation and brings it to a climax by an appeal to the fiction of moral and psychological enquiry. She demands, in the end, a response from the reader which he cannot give, because he cannot feel that the solution admissable in one mode of fiction can solve the problems raised in another. She tries to conceal this final transition from tragedy to serenity by her commentary: 'It would be a poor result of all our anguish, if we won nothing but our old selves at the end of it—if we could return to the same blind loves, the same self-confident blame, the same light thoughts of human suffering. . . . Let us be thankful that sorrow lives in us as an indestructible force. . . .' But what she is building up in her commentary, George Eliot is destroying in her narrative; we see intention outstripping imagination, the moralist 'filling-in' for the artist. Hetty's tragedy does not exist in the world of Adam's marriage; to accept the reality of one is to reject the other. In a letter about *Adam Bede*, George Eliot writes: 'The whole course of the story . . . the description of scenery and houses—the characters—the dialogue—*everything* is a combination from widely sundered elements of experience. . . .' I would suggest that the elements remained sundered; the gap between the world of descriptions and the world of analysis is never bridged so that 'one begins to suspect at length that there is no direct connection between eyelashes and morals. . . .'

The final interest of *Adam Bede* is that it casts its shadow before it. No single novel has the kind of decisive impact that alters the course of fiction, but some novels reveal, consciously or otherwise, a pattern of conflict which later generations come to see as marking a notable change in the art of fiction. Perhaps the novel itself had little influence in such a determination, but looking back we can see that it embodied one in however rudimentary a way. Occasionally we do have a particular novel which seems a landmark in the history of fiction, setting up new possibilities for the artist, but novels like *Emma* and *A la Recherche du Temps Perdu* are extremely rare. Looking at the fiction of George Eliot we feel that it both sums up all that has been done in the world of English fiction before then and yet contains within it the seeds of what is to come. In her best work, *Middlemarch*, *Daniel Deronda*, these two elements are clearly discernible. There is the description of a whole social community, presented in such a way that we are asked to look now at this feature and now that. The author's intervention is, in its various tones of voice, an indispensable part of the novel, distancing the fiction and ensuring a certain contemplative response from the reader. In Chapter XVII of the novel George Eliot discourses on her art and remarks that her purpose is 'to give a faithful account of things as they have mirrored themselves in my mind'. The image is an interesting one because it gives a peculiar twist to the kind of 'realism' usually intended by users of the mirror analogy. There is no sense of mere passivity here, of a photographic correspondence between the literary work and the reality which it imitates; the mirror is there, but it is the mirror of a particular mind. Though an interpretation of 'the seen' must be the task of every novelist, George Eliot ensures that it is the form of her novels that will make this quite explicit. She acts both as guide and creator. With James and subsequent fiction the guide had become superannuated, and the reader is left to personal exploration. We no longer look at things so much as find them out. With this shift from contemplation to participation, the subject matter itself has altered; the social community in moral action gives way to the individual consciousness in moral reflection. 'Innocence' is translated into 'integrity'.

Before George Eliot we have Tom Jones and Roderick Random and Mr Knightley and Mr Pickwick; after her we have Gilbert Osmund and Stephen Dedalus and Paul Morel and Marlow. Obviously there are exceptions, but the drift is plain. In her novels we find both genealogies present. In *Middlemarch* she directs us to a 'study of provincial life', and clearly this is an extension of the Hayslope community of *Adam Bede*; but, accompanying this, is her analysis of the egotistic conscience in Casaubon and Dorothea and Fred Vincy and Rosamund, an enquiry which has begun with Adam and Dinah and Arthur and Hetty. The difference between the two novels is not one of kind, but of success in dealing with the kind. The moral drama finds in *Middlemarch* itself a perfect setting and the dictum of *Felix Holt* is convincingly illustrated, 'there is no private life that has not been determined by a wider public life'. With George Eliot these aspects are equally stressed. With James, however, the enquiry into 'the private life', and with it the development of new fictional techniques, begins on a grand scale, and with Lawrence it comes to something like an apotheosis. It is interesting that, looking back, both these novelists see George Eliot's work as marking an end and a beginning. For James, *Middlemarch* 'sets a limit to the old-fashioned English novel', but for Lawrence 'it was really George Eliot who started it all. It was she who started putting all the action inside.' An end and a beginning, an old world and a new—*Adam Bede* in a hesitant and discordant way discloses both, and in doing so marks a distinctive stage, not only in George Eliot's work, but also in the history of English fiction.

[handwritten marginal note: Eliot discloses both old & new world in novel-]

[*Note*]

It would alter the focus of my discussion if I enlarged on this description of the critical reaction, but reference ought to be made here to particular critics, if for no other reason than that I have profited by reading them, though my conclusions are not theirs. In the first group there are those who see *Adam Bede* primarily as a novel of moral enquiry: Jerome Thale, *The Novels of George Eliot*, 1959, Ch. I; Barbara Hardy, *The Novels of George Eliot*, 1959, Ch. II; Albert J. Fyfe, 'The Interpretation of Adam Bede', *Nineteenth-Century Fiction*, 1954. In the second group there are those who see the novel as belonging primarily to a pastoral convention: Van Ghent, *The English Novel: Form and Function*, 'Adam Bede' 1953; G. C. Creeger, 'An Interpretation of Adam Bede' *E.L.H.* 1956; Maurice Hussey, 'Structure and Imagery in Adam Bede', *Nineteenth-Century Fiction*, 1955; R. A. Foakes, ' "Adam Bede" Reconsidered', *English*, 1959.

From Ian Gregor and Brian Nicholas, *The Moral and the Story*, 1962, 'The Two Worlds of Adam Bede (1859)', pp. 13–32 (13, 17–20, 24, 26, 28–32).

CAROLE ROBINSON

Romola : A Reading of the Novel

It is easy to misread *Romola*, and if we do we shall not understand why it is so remarkable a failure. Its ostensible theme (too easily summarized as 'the contrast or conflict between unscrupulous egotism and self-sacrificing devotion to duty'), and the beautification of its heroine (too quickly dismissed as 'the proclamation of her author's ethical ideals[1]), lend the novel an air of Victorian moral assurance which scrutiny will discover to be a façade. 'Egotism' and 'devotion' are themes of *Romola*, but they are not so simply explored as the contrasting destinies of Tito and Romola imply. If that contrast were all that motivated the novel, then the novel would be insufferable indeed. 'The singing progress to Paradise on the one hand, the stuttering descent to Hell on the other'— D. H. Lawrence's phrase from *The Rainbow*—*almost* describes the crossed paths of the heroine and the villain, but not quite. Tito goes to Hell surely enough; but despite Romola's rippling halo, there is no singing in her progress to Paradise; indeed, there is no paradise, but only a long purgatory. The true conflicts of *Romola* occur within the heroine, not between heroine and villain.

The motif of choice is essential to *Romola*. Criticism deals with it always where it is dullest, in relation to Tito. Tito's choices are simple; between obvious good and obvious evil he consistently chooses evil. Romola's choices are difficult because she herself has to determine anew the value of established sanctions, or else determine whose authority she may accept. For example, with regard to the marriage contract, she leaves Tito, then accepts Savonarola's injunction that she return; leaves him again, and in a sense returns again to rear his illegitimate children. While no suspense attaches to Tito's deterioration, each of Romola's decisions involves a crisis. Thus while Tito is merely tiresome, Romola is exhausting.

Probably George Eliot intended Romola to be a moral exemplar; but we have only to remember that Romola makes an ambiguous attempt at suicide, after suffering an extraordinary history of perplexities, to suspect that she ended by embodying a despair beyond what her author intended for her. George Eliot is in fact lyrically evasive on this point of 'suicide': 'The clear waves seemed to invite her: she wished she could lie down to sleep on them and pass from sleep into death. But Romola could not directly seek death; the fullness of young life in her forbade that. She could only wish that death would come.'[2] 'Drifting Away' is an euphemistic title for this chapter whose final two paragraphs openly recognize Romola's eagerness to die. Unlike Maggie Tulliver, Romola does not find death by water. In the earlier novel the novelist admitted her failure to find another solution to her heroine's dilemmas; in *Romola* George Eliot makes a more strenuous effort at affirmation. In a later work, The *Spanish Gipsy*, the question recurs, since Fedalma too contemplates what Camus has called 'the one truly serious philosophical problem': 'Judging whether life is or is not worth living amounts to answering the fundamental question of philosophy. And . . . you can appreciate the importance of that reply, for it will precede the

---

[1] Gerald Bullet, *George Eliot: Her Life and Books*, New Haven 1948, pp. 214, 215.

[2] *Romola*, ch. LXI. All quotes from the novels are from *The Works of George Eliot*, Cabinet Edition.

definitive act.'[3] The absence of a definitive act in *Romola* perhaps indicates the uncertainty of George Eliot's reply to the question to which Camus directs us.

Indeed, philosophic uncertainty is the keynote of the novel, and the source of *Romola*'s failure is to be sought not in its moral intentions or its didacticism, but in doubt, and in the novelist's uncertain faith in the affirmations she proposes in her effort to satisfy doubt. *Romola* is not so much a novel as an essay in uncertainties. The repetitive plot pattern of commitment and disillusion, decision and indecision, may then be attributed to the novelist's dissatisfaction with the solutions she proposes for the heroine, and not, as Mrs Hardy suggests[4], to artistry and design. The heroine is readily identified with the Victorian intellectual. Her problems of doubt and despair have a later than *quattrocento* ring, and the Victorian intelligentsia responded with particular fervour to *Romola*.

The novel anticipates even the modern wasteland, whose familiar images, we hear in Dino's prophecy: 'And thou, Romola, didst wring thy hands and seek for water, and there was none . . . and the plain was bare and stony again, and thou wast alone in the midst of it' (ch. xv); and in Romola's fulfilment of it: 'the springs were all dried up around her; she wondered what other waters there were at which men drank and found strength in the desert' (ch. xxxvi). And if the Victorian philosophy of compromise has been replaced by a modern one of crisis', it is the latter mood which *Romola*, with its 'life of unrelieved grand crisis', as Barbara Hardy calls it (p.61), exemplifies. Indeed, a complex of themes—isolation, doubt, freedom, anxiety, flight—makes the novel curiously familiar, so that if George Eliot had acknowledged, and not disguised, the novel's implications, *Romola* would perhaps have been the manifesto of a Victorian existentialism.

I

Romola was largely written in 1862, five years before the passage of the second Reform Bill inaugurated the modern era in politics; and the novel is of modern rather than medieval interest. The historical apparatus over which George Eliot laboured with so Victorian an assiduity may probably be ignored for all but its Victorian connotations. Carlyle's diametric poles, 'past' and 'present', coalesce in the historical novel. The Florentine scene provides, inconsistently enough, both in analogy of and a criterion for, George Eliot's own society. What Carlyle found in the world of the medieval monastry, an example of fruitful community, George Eliot intermittently finds in Florence: 'a narrow scene of corporate action . . . a community shut in close by the hills and by walls of six miles' circuit, where men knew each other as they passed in

[3] Albert Camus, *The Myth of Sisyphus*, trans. Justin O'Brien, New York 1955, p. 30.
[4] Barbara Hardy, *The novels of George Eliot*, London 1959, p. 61.

the street, set their eyes every day on the memorials of their common-wealth' ('Proem'). Communal rituals, rather self-consciously empha-sized, correspond to the rustic choruses of the English novels: fairs, a sermon, political assemblages, processions of religious celebration or supplication. These last especially intend a judgment on communal expressions: 'There has been no great people without processions' (ch. VIII). There is of course, a good deal of Victorian nostalgia in this presentation of Florence as a community bound by ceremonies, organic, and possessing a communal voice, in contrast to the fragmentizing society of the industrial era which found its philosophy in atomistic utilitarianism. But alongside this idealization there is another, more realistic mood, which draws a society closer in temper to the Victorian: materialistic, competitive, somewhat vulgar, and portentous with internal contradictions.

In the following, for example, do we not discern the novelist's sense of Victorian complacency, and her equally Victorian premonition of social upheaval?

At the close of 1492. . . . Italy was enjoying a peace and prosperity unthreatened by any near and definite danger. There was no fear of famine, for the seasons had been plenteous in corn, and wine, and oil; new palaces had been rising in all fair cities, new villas on pleasant slopes and summits; and the men who had more than their share of these good things were in no fear of the larger number who had less. . . .

Altogether this world, with its partitioned empire and its roomy universal Church, seemed to be a handsome establishment for the few who were lucky or wise enough to reap the advantages of human folly. . . . The heavens were fair and smiling above; and below there were no signs of earthquake. (ch. XXI).

The biblical language of the first passage seems an invitation to read it as a parable; while the second passage, with its 'empire', 'Church', and 'handsome establishment' works to confirm our Victorian associations. Florence is like England, beset by Mammon; this Florentine burgher might be done by Thackeray; 'he loved his honours and his gains, the business of his counting-house, of his guild, of the public council-chamber. . . . He loved to strengthen his family by a good alliance' ('Proem'). The chief triumphal car in the procession of St John is that of the Zecca, or Mint, 'for where could the image of the patron saint be more fitly placed than on the symbol of the Zecca?' (ch. VIII). There is here no denunciation in the manner of Carlyle or Ruskin, but it is almost impossible to imagine that these analogies are false.

II

There are political analogies as well. The death of Lorenzo the Magnificent has left a void of authority, and among the competing factions which arise is Savonarola's popular party, which demands a Great Council 'giving an expression to the public will large enough to counteract the vitiating influence of party interests' (ch. xxxv). Although Savonarola is George Eliot's only possible 'hero', her attitude towards his party is ambivalent; and her treatment of Florentine politics reflects Victorian political apprehensions. The people of Florence are eager for 'some unknown good which they called liberty' (ch. xxix). A cynic calls popular government the 'triumph of the fat popolani over the lean, which again means triumph of the fattest popolano over those who are less fat' (ch. viii). The Mediceans see the political alternative as lying between riotous democracy and orderly oligarchy: 'there are but two sorts of government: one where men show their teeth at each other, and one where men show their tongues and lick the feet of the strongest' (ch. xxxix). This political conservatism, which George Eliot seems to endorse despite her admiration for Savonarola, must be seen in the light of Victorian social awareness and guilt. Several times while writing *Romola*, in 1862, George Eliot mentioned in letters to the Brays her concern about the distresses of textile workers in Coventry, affected by the cotton famine caused by the American civil war. In a letter to M. D'Albert-Durade she spoke of 'hoping, for the sake of Lancashire weavers out of work, that the winter will not be severe.'[5] The faces Tito sees in the crowd he harangues are those of 'weavers and dyers' (ch. xxix), and in one episode Romola must defend herself against a hungry and impatient mob of labourers.

Raymond Williams analyses this bourgeois Victorian fear of social violence in his discussion of the industrial novels.[6] The same apprehension underlies a comment such as this one on the economic duress in Florence: 'that large body of the working men who were not counted as citizens and had not so much as a vote to serve as anodyne to their stomachs were likely to get impatient' (ch. xxv). But a more wistful picture of the working man as possibly sober, moderate, and informed—an idea which originates with Adam Bede and culminates in Felix Holt—finds Florentine embodiment in Niccolo the blacksmith: 'the impression of enormous force which was conveyed by his capacious chest and brawny arms . . . was deepened by the keen sense and quiet resolution expressed in his glance and in every furrow of his cheek and brow' (ch. i). Although one assumes he will play a major role, Niccolo's function ends with the utterance of some cautious, and therefore exemplary, *sententiae*: 'I vote and I speak when there's any use in it: if there's hot metal on the anvil, I lose no time before I strike; but I don't spend good hours in tinkling on cold iron' (Ch. i).

George Eliot's comment that during these difficult days 'there was all the more reason that the Republic should keep its religious festivals' (ch. viii), recalls the Victorian unwillingness to sacrifice the church as a social bulwark. Without these 'ancient symbols' (a spectator at the

[5] *The George Eliot Letters*, ed. Gordon S. Haight, IV, 68, New Haven 1955.
[6] *Culture and Society, 1780-1950*, London 1958, Pt. I ch.v.

procession of St John's remarks), 'the vulgar would be conscious of nothing beyond their own petty wants of back and stomach, and never rise to the sense of community in religion and law' (ch. VIII). At holiday time 'the preaching in the Duomo could least of all be dispensed with' (ch. XXII), and thus even the radical Savonarola is commended by his enemies as being 'firm as a rock on that point of promoting peace' (ch. XXXIX). The estimate in *Romola* of human, and especially lower-class, nature's ability to exercise its own control, is slight indeed.

There are several contradictions in George Eliot's treatment of Florence, what we may call the public theme of her novel. There is no recognition, much less reconciliation, of the disparity between the idealization of 'community' and the more realistic appraisal of the community itself. . . . The idealization of 'community' is further vitiated by George Eliot's inability to accept the political corollary which Savonarola advances; and even more by the intermittent cynicism regarding human nature which she allows herself to express *at the same time* that she applauds Savonarola's idealism. Perhaps it is an inherent contradiction of Victorian conservatism that while it seeks to deny the atomistic view of society by advancing an ideal of organic connection and community, it leans towards a quite pessimistic estimate of individual possibilities. It was perhaps just this difficulty, of finding a real community to exemplify the abstract idea of community which both her own intellectual impulses and the urgings of Frederic Harrison prompted her to embody in literature, which leads George Eliot in the later works to seek that ideal in ever vaguer 'objective correlatives,' the imaginary African homeland in *The Spanish Gipsy* and the then still visionary Zionist state in *Daniel Deronda*.

III

Since it was George Eliot's conviction that there is no private life which has not been determined by a wider public life, we may expect Romola's history to be as agitated as that of Florence. A history, like Maggie Tulliver's, of a series of difficult relationships with men, its conflicts are nevertheless more strictly intellectual . . . At the climax of the novel, . . . Romola is . . . in flight, . . . in a state of despair and freedom. Under Savonarola's influence she had learned to 'reject her impulsive choice,' to 'obey passively the guidance of outward claims' (ch. LII); but this external prop and moral standard, first invested in her father and then in Savonarola, has again been removed, and Romola must face her existentialist dilemma alone. Her reaction, and George Eliot's, is at first an outright evasion: that almost comical escape to the sea by which she hopes 'to be freed from the burden of choice . . . to commit herself, sleeping, to destiny which would either bring death or else new necessities that might rouse a new life in her!' (ch. LXI). Now comes the bleakest avowal of Romola's position: 'She was alone now: she had freed herself from all claims, she had freed herself even from that burden of choice which presses with heavier and heavier weight when claims have loosed their guiding hold' (ch. LXI).

Romola's voyage is the existentialist leap, that crisis of the existentialist drama which comes when at the brink of the 'abyss of freedom' man plunges into the darkness seeking some form of commitment. The scene is absurd; but perhaps the 'absurd' is appropriate in a novel which makes so near an approach to a representation of modern anxiety. Romola feels 'orphaned in those wide spaces of sea and sky,' and the 'far-off symbolic writing of the heavens' holds 'no message of love for her' (ch. LXI). The circumstances to which Romola awakens are, appropriately enough, those of 'the plague'. The remorseless plot resurrects her to a new life of labour, a renewed search for a form of commitment so compelling that her absorption in it will be unreflecting.

The novel can no longer explore its theme; it cannot afford another revulsion in the heroine's feelings. It is brought to a rapid resolution. Romola among the plague-ridden achieves apotheosis again as a blessed Madonna, and finds strength to return to Florence, where she adopts Tito's illegitimate family. Reassuming all obligations, she reigns at the end of the novel a 'queen' without a consort, like Fedalma; and like George Eliot herself (oddly called Madonna in her later life, and 'Mutter' to the sons of Agnes Lewes), a childless Mother. The epilogue is as calm as the novel was agitated. A female placidity prevails, with Romola the presiding matriarch.

IV

It is possible that any attempt George Eliot might have made to resolve the turbulence of *Romola* would have been unacceptable; but that which lies in the alliance of Romola and Tessa, and the suppression of the disturbing masculine element, seems peculiarly evasive, since it resolves Romola's search for a standard of authority simply by establishing her as the only authority remaining in the novel. The 'Queen' and 'Madonna' imagery which surrounds Romola becomes oppressive not because it betrays the novelist's partiality for, or identification with, the heroine, but because it represents the false resolution of a true dilemma. Thus, Elizabeth Bowen's dictum, that the 'moral angle' of a novel must proceed from the novelist's 'certainty of the validity of the truth the novel is to present'[7] is the most pertinent standard one may apply to *Romola*; for our judgment of its failure depends upon our dissatisfaction with the novelist's mode of answering the questions she raises: 'whom to believe' and 'what to do'. There is perhaps only one truth in *Romola* of which George Eliot is convinced, a melancholy fable hidden amidst affirmations; and that is the fact of Romola's confusion, isola-

---

[7] 'Notes on Writing a Novel' in *Modern Literary Criticism*, ed. Irving Howe, Boston 1958, p. 59.

tion and despair, a mood in which the validity even of her own emotions is eventually called into question.

We come round again to intellectual history, for these aspects of the failure of the novel are of an order of contradiction found elsewhere in Victorian literature. Romola is a heroine without God and thus, in terms of the Feuerbachian theology which George Eliot substituted for orthodoxy, she must and does seek God in man. But man—her father, her husband, her brother, her spiritual guide—disappoints her. (Here George Eliot must qualify continually, must mitigate the disillusion which allows nothing to remain, neither God nor God-in-man.) The same contradiction inheres in the public theme: George Eliot endorses Savonarola's plan of community and love, but a Medicean scoffs at those who 'want to make believe we can all love each other' (ch. xxxix). Does he voice the realism which rose in the novelist's own argumentative mind?

Again, the great apostasy of Feuerbachian theology must lie in failure of feeling, for when God ceases to be an objective reality, then emotion, the subjective reality of the heart, alone justifies human existence. 'Feeling' is the critical term in *The Essence of Christianity*. Thus doubts of the validity of one's fellow-feeling may be as critical as religious guilt. George Eliot is too honest not to note Romola's failings along these lines, her lack of true involvement in her communal labours; her 'sense of defect in her devotedness' to her father, which 'made her cling with all the force of compunction as well as affection to the duties of memory'. (ch. xxviii). On the other hand, George Eliot must insist on the values with which she is left, on the remaining, fully human, sanctities. Thus there comes about an overemphasis upon Romola's 'keen fellow-feeling,' which the character in her actual relationships is unable to demonstrate. Tito is produced to display the immorality of those not touched by personal and communal loyalties, but Romola emerges from the particular intellectual tensions which underlie her conception equally detached.

In writing *Romola* George Eliot wrestled with conflicts and uncertainties peculiar to her day, and if she was compelled as a teacher to pluck affirmation from among the nettles of intellectual perplexities, in a moment of truth she justified her procedure: 'these beings unvisited by angels had no other choice than to grasp that stumbling guidance along the path of reliance and action which is the path of life, or else to pause in loneliness and disbelief, which is no path, but the arrest of inaction and death' (ch. xxxvi). Perhaps finally we may consider *Romola*, with its massive erudition camouflaging its uncertainties, a revealing achievement of the Victorian spirit, and a memorial to its determination to make labour compensate for the absence of belief.

From *Victorian Studies*, Vol. 6, September 1962, pp. 29–42 (29–35, 40–2).

H

DAVID R. CARROLL

'Silas Marner: Reversing the Oracles of Religion'

Silas Marner is usually treated as a successful and uncomplicated
jeu d'esprit written by a George Eliot recuperating from the anguished
cul-de-sac of The Mill on the Floss and preparing for the intellectual
labours which were to result in Romola. Her own comments have
probably encouraged this response to the work: 'It came to me first of
all, quite suddenly, as a sort of legendary tale, suggested by my recollection of having once, in early childhood, seen a linen weaver with a bag
on his back; but, as my mind dwelt on the subject, I became inclined to
a more realistic treatment.'[1] In reality, Silas Marner is carefully built
around a structure of ideas which were of the utmost concern to George
Eliot, and it forms a vital link in the logic of her development as a
novelist. It is the very simplicity that has led to the persistent under-
valuation of the novel. The magical and fairy-tale elements of the story
have been accepted as the substance rather than the vehicle of George
Eliot's meaning, and the novel has been considered most suitable for
generations of school-children. The best way to redress this under-
valuation is to define the rigorously intellectual structure upon which the
novel is built; only then can the subversive and explosive nature of
George Eliot's conclusions be fully grasped.

I

Silas Marner consists of two separate stories, those of Silas himself and
of Godfrey Cass. These two stories, which are given equal weight in the
novel, interlock briefly but crucially . . . at the climax of the novel . . .
the two worlds of the novel confront each other; the protagonists,
conscious of their past defeats and triumphs, vehemently debate the
ownership of Eppie which they both now recognize to be crucial.
Godfrey and Nancy first say they would like to adopt Eppie in order
to 'make a lady of her'. When Eppie rejects this offer, Godfrey asserts
his legal claim: 'But I've a claim on you, Eppie—the strongest of all
claims. It's my duty, Marner, to own Eppie as my child, and provide
for her. She's my own child; her mother was my wife. I've a natural
claim on her that must stand before every other.' Silas rejects Godfrey's
interpretation of the word 'natural': '. . . then, sir, why didn't you say so

[1] The George Eliot Letters, ed. Gordon S. Haight, III, 382.

sixteen years ago, and claim her before I'd come to love her . . .? God gave her to me because you turned your back upon her, and He looks upon her as mine. You've no right to her. When a man turns a blessing from his door, it falls to them as take it in.' At the impasse, the final decision is left to Eppie, and already in the name given to her by Silas there is an anticipation of her verdict. Eppie is a shortened form of Hephzibah, and Silas with his 'It's a Bible name' (chap. XIV) directs us to Isaiah's address to Jerusalem: 'Thou shalt no more be termed Forsaken; neither shall thy land and more be termed Desolate; but thou shalt be called Hephzibah, and thy land Beulah; for the Lord delighteth in thee, and thy land shall be married.'[2] These words are a reassurance to Silas that his instinctive affection for Eppie will not be betrayed.

The arrival of the Casses at the cottage had broken in upon Silas' discussion of this very subject with Eppie . . . Eppie's reply, postponed by the knock at the door, comes now at the climax of the debate which has helped to clarify her attitude. In the oblique discussion on ownership and legality in the Rainbow no final solution was reached, and indeed the whole conversation was interrupted by the sudden arrival of the desolate Silas seeking help. Now, sixteen years later, when the same problems are raised, Eppie can provide a solution, and she is able to do so because of her relationship with Silas during these sixteen years. These years of dependence and affection are the all-important factor. Godfrey is trying to go back sixteen years to the moment when he rejected Eppie, and carry on from there. But the growing dependence of Silas upon her love has come to overlay and cancel Godfrey's claim. She rejects his claim in these words: 'We've been used to be happy together every day, and I can't think o' no happiness without him. And he says he'd nobody i' the world till I was sent to him, and he'd have nothing when I was gone. And he's took care of me and loved me from the first, and I'll cleave to him as long as he lives, and nobody shall ever come between him and me . . . I can't feel as I've got any father but one'. . . .

Eppie's rejection finally brings home to Godfrey the inescapable consequences of his actions. He grasps now the crucial truism that when he denied Eppie he not only ignored her claims but he also allowed other claims to be made on her. Silas's increasing claims have invalidated his own purely legal parenthood. As Godfrey himself vividly expresses it: 'While I've been putting off and putting off, the trees have been growing: it's too late now'. (ch. XX) This is the last obstacle to Godfrey's regeneration; he now appreciates fully his wife's love and accepts his childlessness with resignation. . . . The . . . importance of the structural division of the novel into two discrete stories lies here. This division creates a clearly defined area of mystery at the centre of the novel in which the protagonists can exercise their myth-making faculties. Silas and Godfrey are each isolated within their own halves of the novel; Silas has brief glimpses of the rich Cass family, and Godfrey

[2] *Isaiah*, LXII 4 . . .

is dimly aware of Silas's existence. Then the two worlds briefly inter-act: Dunstan steals Silas's gold, and Silas adopts Godfrey's child. Because of the separation of the stories, these interlockings are mys-terious and apparently inexplicable. The reader watches omnisciently to see how the two characters will react to these mysterious interventions in their lives. They react, inevitably, by creating their own mythical explanations. Thus, in *Silas Marner*, George Eliot is not only evaluating the established myths of Christianity; she also domesticates the theme and dramatizes the private myth-making of the main characters.

The significance of the mysterious interlockings comes out clearly if one examines the characters' reactions. The first impingement on Silas's private world occurs after fifteen years of solitude when his gold is stolen. Because he is solitary and embittered, he assumes that the all-powerful, alien God of Lantern Yard had again intervened in his life: '*Was* it a thief who had taken the bags? Or was it a cruel power that no hands could reach which had delighted in making him a second time desolate?' (ch. v). Without love and trust the world must remain inexplicable and haphazard. The second impingement of the Casses' world upon Silas's soon follows. When Eppie arrives, Silas again makes no attempt to penetrate the ara of mystery by seeking a rational explana-tion: '. . . he formed no conjectures of ordinary natural means by which the event could have been brought about' (ch. XII). But an important difference soon appears. Although it is equally inexplicable, Silas does not dismiss this second intervention as the meaningless act of vengeful God. Thanks to his growing love for Eppie, he begins to suspect that there is an order present in the universe in which he can trust. We see him tentatively formulating a myth expressive of this new confidence: 'Thought and feeling were so confused within him, that if he had tried to give them utterance, he could only have said that the child was come instead of his gold—that the gold has turned into the child.' (ch. XIV). This explanation, this myth is superior to his previous surrender to an inexplicable, miraculous God because here there is an attempt to find an order and a logic in events. This is leading him towards, not away from, the complex universe; and George Eliot implies that Silas's myth of order does embody a psychological truth—his gold-centred world has to be destroyed so that his love could flourish. This personal myth-making, this private search for order, is the crucial transitional phase in Silas's career between the destruction of his old religious faith and the complete acceptance of a new one.

The same strategy is used in Godfrey's regeneration. The impinge-ments of Silas's world upon his are at first explained away as further manifestations of Chance. There is no attempt to find any logical con-nections between the two worlds: 'To connect the fact of Dunsey's dis-appearance with that of the robbery occurring on the same day, lay quite away from the track of every one's thoughts—even Godfrey's, who had better reason than anyone else to know what his brother was capable of' (ch. X). Chance like Silas's 'God of lies', becomes more and more powerful in Godfrey's life the more he is lacking in the strength of love. Chance plays into Godfrey's hands a second time and gives him a new start in life when Silas adopts Eppie. Once again, the disparity between the individual and the inexplicable universe is bridged by superstitious and miraculous explanations until love asserts itself and myths of order replace those of chance. Godfrey begins to formulate his myth of order when he and Nancy discover they can't have children of their own: he comes to see his childlessness as a retribution. One can see the culmination of this myth at the final impingement of the two worlds, on the discovery of Dunstan and the gold, when what appears to be the most fortuitous event in the novel is seen by Godfrey as the judicial act of an all-powerful God. This is not the end of his regeneration but it is leading him towards and not away from life's complexities; and, as in Silas's case, Godfrey's new myth embodies a psychological truth—the all-powerful God who uncovered the sixteen-year-old mystery was, in fact, his own love for his wife acting surreptitiously. As the two main characters create more valid mythical explanations in this way, they are moving further and further across the area of mystery between the two stories, to the final debate where they come to understand the nature of their interrelationship.

This is the function of the structural division of the novel. It creates an area of mystery which George Eliot says is an inescapable condition of human existence. This area is the testing-ground of the protagonists' myth-making faculties and within it George Eliot demonstrates that valid myths of order are a direct expression of love, while invalid myths of chance result from an absence of love. The former act as intermediaries between the individual and the realities of life, and the latter seek to deny these realities. The materials out of which these myths are created in the novel are the traditional symbols of the gold coins, the golden-haired child, New Year's Eve, the death caused by the gold, the cataleptic fits, and so on. Critics of *Silas Marner* have pursued the meaning of the novel through endless symbolic permutations of these elements without realizing that the important thing is to see what the characters themselves make of this material. George Eliot is simply suggesting that when the individual is not strengthened by love then the combination of life's elements can only appear to him fortuitous; but when strengthened by love, he makes out of them a pattern, a meaning, which is a mythical, but faithful expression of his own experience. Love, in each case determines the meaning of life. And here, as love turns into God, we have the ultimate reversal of the oracles of religion in the novel.[3]

In *Silas Marner*, George Eliot examines the variety of myths created by her characters in response to the mystery of the worlds in which they live. An awareness of this central theme enables us to place the novel firmly in the mainstream of George Eliot's development. We can see

---

[3] [Cf. Feuerbach, *The Essence of Christianity*, trans. G. Eliot, Harper Torchbooks, New York 1957, p. 271]

her beginning to generalize more freely about the individual's encounter with a complex reality, and to create quickly and order naturally a variety of responses to this encounter. George Eliot moves so confidently here because in *Silas Marner* she is still in the world of the traditional communities of her early novels. But this is the last occasion on which she takes over the rooted, instinctively accepted structure of symbol and belief of such a community, and uses it with subtle re-orientation and economy to express her own meaning. . . .

George Eliot's confidence in creating and manipulating the different mythologies of this novel points ahead to *Middlemarch* where essentially the same method is used on a far larger scale and with much greater diversity. In this later novel, George Eliot has moved outside the bounds of the traditional communities so that the myths by which the characters live are not limited to varieties of religious belief; now, as well as Bulstrode's egocentric Methodism, we have Caleb Garth's religion of 'business' and Mrs. Cadwallader's myth of 'blood'. But, despite this greater diversity, the use and assessment of these myths is the same. George Eliot is again intent on showing the irreducible core of human affection at the centre of valid mythologies; and Dorothea Brooke's search for the key to all the mythologies of Middlemarch society, and her gradual and painful discoveries, are a sophisticated version of those of the main characters in *Silas Marner*. And in nothing does this kinship show itself more clearly than in George Eliot's use of structure to create and assess the various myths created by the characters. The structural innovation of *Silas Marner*, the division of the novel into two separate stories, provides the area of mystery which the characters seek to explain by their myths; and, at the same time, this division is the instrument by which George Eliot isolates the vital factor essential to any valid myth. . . . The structural innovation of dividing this novel into several self-contained social worlds reflects the fragmentary form of Middlemarch society, and at the same time challenges the characters to create personal myths which will make a meaningful whole out of this complexity. These myths are then tested, modified, or rejected by the developing unity of the novel. It is in this perspective that the success and importance of *Silas Marner* must be determined.

From Eric Rothstein, and Thomas K. Dunseath (eds), *Literary Monographs*, Vol. 1, The University of Wisconsin Press, 1967, pp. 167–200 (167, 193–200).

Scenes of Clerical Life

. . . 'Janet's Repentance' . . . achieves in a limited fashion what George Eliot's first two stories failed to accomplish; it depicts a time-bound world in which transcending ideals are still possible. Though it repeats the elements in 'Amos Barton,' it corrects their imbalance and disproportion. The town of Milby, rather than the single figure of Amos, is now the object of the author's satire; Janet and the contrite Milbyites who follow the casket of a near-saint, rather the mourners of Milly Barton, dramatize the novelist's creed; the death of a genuinely 'ideal character,' and not that of any overworked housewife, exemplifies the basic values of that creed. Like Amelia and Caterina, the minister dies to teach us the 'sad weakness' that 'the thought of a man's death hallows him anew to us; as if life were not sacred too' (ch. XI, p. 176).[1]

All three *Scenes of Clerical Life* rely on this melancholy truism. The deaths of Captain Wybrow and Lawyer Dempster act as ironic reminders of a man's vulnerability to time; the ambitions of both, their past promises and expectations, come to naught. But death also reminds man of his duty to sanctify the present: 'the angels come to visit us, and we only know them when they are gone' (ch. V, p. 109). Milly Barton and Mr. Tyran are two such angels in human form; their deaths are meant to bring about a purification. Even Caterina Gilfil's premature death is intended to produce a wider sympathy for her husband; pity, but also fear, are to be extracted from a 'drama of hope and love' long since buried by layers of time. Yet the death of Edward Tryan has the widest effect; there is a greater sense of catharsis and a feeling of completion and rededication. Unlike the deaths of Amelia and Caterina, his end marks a triumph over his temporal self. The clergyman who was afraid of losing 'so much time,' of leaving 'nothing done at all,' becomes the most adequate vehicle for that 'awe and pity' which George Eliot wanted to stimulate in her three novellas.

This awe and pity, however, are not those of tragedy. Tryan's death is that of a martyr; it is exemplary and pathetic rather than dramatic. The story's dramatic movement is provided by Janet's inner conversion and not by her passive observation of another's Christ-like passion. The matured Janet comes to admit that the world she has deprecated is not devoid of love and purpose. But her conversion is still rendered sentimentally, still marked by those teardrops which according to Feuerbach, 'mirror the nature of the Christian's God.'[2] George Eliot was now ready for the larger canvas of *Adam Bede*. In it she tried to justify the

[1] All references to Cabinet edition.
[2] Feuerbach, *The Essence of Christianity*, p. 61.

tragedy of man's fall without resorting to the sentimentality of her three *Scenes of Clerical Life*. Amos Barton, Maynard Gilfil, and Janet Demp-ster accept their fates through the tearful deaths of others; Adam Bede learns how to bear his lot directly through his own experience. Although he, too, is affected by extraneous events such as his father's death and Hetty's degradation, in his strength and self-reliance he seems less passive than George Eliot's previous three protagonists. Like Mr. Tryan, the son of Thias the carpenter emulated the second Adam; yet unlike Mr. Tryan, he is allowed to live.

George Eliot had learned much from her experimentations in the *Scenes of Clerical Life*. In the course of writing her three novellas she had significantly shifted her initial objectives. Though they were planned after the model of Balzac's 'scenes de la vie de province,'[2] her stories had moved from the scientific 'étude' of Barton's grotesque ministry to an attack on the short-sightedness of those who would filter out imperishable essences through their 'scientific lenses' (ch. XI, p. 169). George Eliot was no longer the rationalist of the *Westminster Review*. 'Janet's Repentance' is replete with sarcastic allusions to the 'ingenious philosophers of our own day,' those Benthamites prescribing felicity according to 'arithmetical proportions' (ch. XXII, p. 252). The 'philosophic doctors,' the narrator claims, see the world only in material terms. But there are hidden processes which are 'mysterious,' in-calculable: 'Ideas are often poor ghosts; our sun-filled eyes cannot discern them. . . . But sometimes they are made flesh' (ch. XIX, p. 236). 'Janet's Repentance' thus illustrates a curious reversal. The satirical naturalist who had presented both the poet Young and Amos Barton as inferior 'animals' belonging to the 'species divine' is no longer in evidence. Instead, the narrator of 'Janet's Repentance' turns on an imaginary critic of Mr. Tryan's Evangelical faith, a critic who, sur-prisingly enough, employs the same vocabulary as the narrator of 'Amos Barton.' From his 'bird's-eye station' this myopic critic stereotypes Mr. Tryan: 'Not a remarkable specimen; the anatomy and habits of his species have been determined long ago.' But the critic is immediately accused of presumption by the narrator: 'Our subtlest analysis of schools and sects must miss the essential truth unless it be lit up by the love that sees in all forms of human thought and work, the life-and-death struggles of separate human beings,' (ch. X, pp. 165–6).

[2] In a review written only five months before she began 'Amos Barton,' George recommended *La Folle du Logis* by Leon Gozlan to the admirers of *Scènes de la Vie de Province*. Her description of Gozlan's book applies equally well to 'Amos Barton.': 'It is an entomological tragi-comedy which has many parodies in human society—parodies which Balzac, of all artists, best loved to describe; witness his incomparable *Curé de Tours*, 'Story of a Blue-Bottle', *Leader*, VI [26 April 1856], 401. In 'Brother Jacob,' which like, 'Amos Barton,' relies on the grotesque aspirations of its protagonist, she again alludes to Balzac. Her familiarity with the French novelist, evident throughout her letters, seems to have been due to the influence of Lewes, who had written two articles on Balzac.

With 'Janet's Repentance' George Eliot began a self-dialogue which acquired far richer overtones in the novels to follow. In a modest fashion, she had already found a way to be artistically true to the double aims of her 'realism.' Yet she remained dissatisfied with the reality of Milby. The actual world—which, as she told Blackwood, was so much more vicious than in her story—still weighed upon her. It is significant that in *Adam Bede* she should leave Milby and return to a remoter past, a Wordsworthian realm of unpetted sheep dogs, speckled hens, and patient cart-horses such as had surrounded Tina's brief regeneration, in order to ease Adam's plight.

In 1857, the year in which George Eliot rounded out her three scenes of clerical life, Herman Melville published *The Confidence Man: His Masquerade*. In that obscure fantasy he mocked the secular optimism which in America and in Europe had supplanted the waning religions of the past. The old faith in a Divine Chronometer had been replaced by a belief in the human horologe. But the new belief had altered the shape of the universe; it denied evil; it deliberately ignored the distinct possibility that beyond the veil masking men's existence there might simply be nothing at all. Melville, in the words of a perceptive commentator, regarded the new optimism as but 'a confidence-game played, as it were, by mankind on itself.'[3] Like Melville, George Eliot could no longer believe in a Divine Chronometer. But unlike him, she shrank from the full terror of accounting for the nature of evil in a universe without design. Melville exploited the terror of disorder in his fiction; he played with the ambiguities of life and mocked the 'confidence' of those who projected their own wishes on the universe. George Eliot wanted to temper her own fear of a 'measurable reality' which seemed anarchic and without purpose; to do so, she measured life by a human horologe. 'Janet's Repentance' was her first successful attempt in this direction. But despite the story's forceful ending, the author betrayed her lack of confidence. She had not dispelled her horror over Milby. And, like Janet, she was too honest to keep up 'the old pretence of being happy and satisfied.'

From: *George Eliot's Early Novels: The Limits of Realism*, University of California Press, Berkeley, 1968, pp. 84–8.

[3] Ernest Tuveson, 'The Creed of the Confidence Man,' *ELH* XXXIII (June 1966) 269.

Select Bibliography

WORKS

STANDARD EDITIONS:

'Cabinet Edition'—*The Works of George Eliot*, 20 vols, William Blackwood and Sons, Edinburgh and London, 1878–80.

Essays of George Eliot, ed. T. Pinney, Routledge, London, 1963.

USEFUL RECENT EDITIONS:

Adam Bede, foreword by F. R. Leavis, Signet, New American Library, New York, 1961.

Daniel Deronda, introduction by F. R. Leavis (which modifies his observations in *The Great Tradition*), Harper Torchbooks, New York, 1961.

Danel Deronda, ed. Barbara Hardy with useful introduction and notes, Penguin English Library, Penguin Books, Harmondsworth, 1967.

Felix Holt, introduction by F. R. Leavis, Everyman Library, Dent, London, 1967.

Middlemarch, ed. G. S. Haight, Riverside Edition, Houghton Mifflin, Boston, 1956.

Middlemarch, ed. W. J. Harvey, Penguin English Library, Penguin, Harmondsworth, 1965.

Silas Marner, ed. Q. D. Leavis, Penguin English Library, Penguin, Harmondsworth, 1967.

The Mill on the Floss, ed. G. S. Haight (good introduction and text), Riverside Edition, Houghton Mifflin, Boston, 1961.

BIBLIOGRAPHIES OF CRITICISM:

J. D. Barry, 'The Literary Reputation of George Eliot's Fiction: A Supplementary Bibliography', *Bulletin of Bibliography*, Vol. 22 no. 8, January–April 1959, pp. 176–82. Supplements late Victorian bibliographies up to the end of 1956.

W. H. Marshall, 'A Selective Bibliography of Writings about George Eliot, to 1965', *Bulletin of Bibliography*, Vol. 25, nos 3 and 4, May–August and September–November 1967, pp. 70–2 and 88–94.

LETTERS AND BIOGRAPHIES:

J. W. Cross, *George Eliot's Life as Related in her Letters and Journals*, 3 vols, William Blackwood and Sons, Edinburgh and London, 1885. The single volume edition (1887) contains additional material.

G. S. Haight, *George Eliot: A Biography*, Oxford University Press London, 1968.

G. S. Haight edited *The George Eliot Letters*, 7 vols, Oxford and Yale, London, 1954–56.

A. T. Kitchel, *George Lewes and George Eliot*, John Day, New York, 1933.

CRITICAL WORKS: (*In addition* to those books and articles from which extracts have been given in this anthology).

(*a*) BOOKS:

J. Bennett, *George Eliot: Her Mind and Her Art*, Cambridge, 1948.

G. Bullett, *George Eliot: Her Life and Books*, London, 1947.

D. R. Carroll, (ed.) *George Eliot: The Critical Heritage*, Routledge, London, 1971. A good, but expensive, selection of criticism up to 1885.

L. J. Clipper, *George Eliot's Silas Marner*, Pennant Key-Indexed Study Guide, Bantam Books, New York, 1966. Contains useful suggestions.

G. W. Cooke, *George Eliot: A Critical Study of her Life, Writings and Philosophy*, London, 1883. Full of penetrating insights.

J. P. Couch, *George Eliot in France: A French Appraisal of George Eliot's writings, 1850-1960*, University of N. Carolina Press, Chapel Hill, 1967.

G. R. Creeger, *George Eliot: A Collection of Critical Essays*, Twentieth Centruy Views, Prentice-Hall, Englewood Cliffs, New Jersey, 1970.

D. Daiches, *George Eliot: Middlemarch*, E. Arnold, Studies in Engl. Lit., Series, London, 1963. A good short book.

G. S. Haight, *A Century of George Eliot Criticism*, Methuen, London, 1966. Highly recommended.

B. Hardy, *The Novels of George Eliot: A Study in Form*, Athlone Press, London, 1964.

(ed.), *Middlemarch: Critical Approaches to the Novel*, Athlone Press, London, 1967, essays by Schorer, Harvey, Beaty, D. Oldfield, Hulme, Hardy and Tompkins.

(ed.), *Critical Essays on George Eliot*, Routledge, London, 1970, essays by D. and S. Oldfield, Goode, Hardy, Haddakin, Levine, Kettle, Armstrong, Martin, Harvey.

W. J. Harvey, *The Art of George Eliot*, Chatto, London, 1961.

J. Holmstrom and L. Lerner, *George Eliot and her readers: A Selection of Contemporary Reviews*, Bodley Head, London, 1966.

R. T. Jones, *A Critical Commentary on George Eliot's 'Adem Bede'*, Macmillan Critical Commentary Series, London, 1968.

A. T. Kitchel, *George Eliot's Quarry for 'Middlemarch'*, Berkeley, 1950.

U. C. Knoepflmacher, *Religious Humanism and the Victorian Novel: George Eliot, Walter Pater, and Samuel Butler*, Princeton U.P., 1970.

F. R. Leavis, *The Great Tradition: George Eliot, Henry James, Joseph Conrad*, Chatto, London, 1948,.

L. D. Lerner, *The Truthtellers: Jane Austen, George Eliot, D. H. Lawrence*, Chatto, London, 1967.

I. Milner, *The Structure of Values in George Eliot*, Prague, 1968.

A. A. Moller, *George Eliots Beschäftigung mit dem Judentum und ihre Stellung zur Judenfrage*, Hamburg, 1934.

T. A. Noble, *George Eliot's 'Scenes of Clerical Life'*, Yale U.P., 1956.

B. J. Paris, *Experiments in Life: George Eliot's Quest for Values*, Wayne St U.P., Detroit, 1965.

R. Stang, *Discussions of George Eliot*, Heath, Boston, 1960.

R. Stump, *Movement and Vision in George Eliot's Novels*, U. of Washington Press, Seattle, 1959.

J. Thale, *The Novels of George Eliot*, Columbia U.P., N.Y., 1959. 'Eliot's darkened world.'

(b) ESSAYS AND ARTICLES:

In most cases these *exclude* those to be found in the anthologies of Carroll, Haight and Hardy.

I. Adam, 'Character and Destiny in George Eliot's Fiction', *Nineteenth-Century Fiction*, Vol. 20, 1965, pp. 127–43.

W. Baker, 'George Eliot's Readings in Nineteenth-Century Jewish Historians: A Note on the Background of *Daniel Deronda*, *Victorian Studies*, Vol. 15, 1972, pp. 463-473.

W. Baker, 'The Kabbalah, Mordecai, and George Eliot's Religion of Humanity', *The Yearbook of English Studies*, Vol.3 , 1973, pp. 216-221.

J. Beaty, '*Daniel Deronda* and the Question of Unity in Fiction', *Victorian Newsletter*, Spring 1959, pp. 16–20.
'History by Indirection: The Era of Reform in *Middlemarch*', *Victorian Studies*, Vol. 1, 1957, pp. 173–9. Reprinted in Haight, *Century of G. Eliot Criticism*.

S. L. Bethell, 'The Novels of George Eliot', *Criterion*, Vol. 18, 1938, pp. 39–57.

D. R. Carroll, 'The Unity of *Daniel Deronda*', *Essays in Criticism*, Vol. 9, pp. 369–80.
'*Felix Holt*: Society as Protagonist', *Nineteenth-Century Fiction*, Vol. 17, 1962, opp. 237–52.

G. R. Creeger, 'An Interpretation of *Adam Bede*', *English Literary History*, Vol. 23, 1956, pp. 218–38.

J. S. Diekhoff, 'The Happy Ending of *Adam Bede*', *English Literary History*, Vol. 3, 1936, pp. 221–7.

Barbara Hardy, 'Implication and Incompleteness: George Eliot's *Middlemarch*', in *The Appropriate Form: An Essay on the Novel*, Athlone Press, London, 1964, pp. 105–31.

D. L. Higdon, 'George Eliot and the Art of the Epigram', *Nineteenth-Century Fiction*, Vol. 25, 1970, pp. 127–51.

R. Hoggart, 'A Victorian Masterpiece', (on *Middlemarch*) *Listener*, 8 March 1962, pp. 407–8.

R. H. Hutton, Unsigned review of *Romola, Spectator*, 18 July 1863, pp. 265–7. Most perceptive. Reprinted in Carroll, Naight and Holmstrom.

H. James, 'The Spanish Gypsy', *The North American Review*, Vol. 107, 1868, pp. 620–35. Reprinted in Haight.
Unsigned review of *Middlemarch, Galaxy*, March 1873, pp. 424–8. Reprinted in Carroll.
Review of Cross's *Life, Atlantic Monthly*, May 1885, Vol. 55, pp. 668–78. Reprinted in Carroll.
See also James on *Daniel Deronda*, frequently reprinted.

G. R. Levine, 'Determinism and Responsibility in the Works of George Eliot', *PMLA*, Vol. 77, 1962, pp. 268–79. Reprinted in Haight.
'Intelligence as Deception: *The Mill on the Floss*', *PMLA*, Vol. 80, 1965, pp. 402–9.

R. S. Lyons, 'The Method of *Middlemarch*'; *Nineteenth-Century Fiction*, Vol. 21, 1966, pp. 35–45.

D. Mansell, 'George Eliot's Conception of Tragedy', *Nineteenth-Century Fiction*, Vol. 22, 1967, pp. 155–71.

M. Y. Mason, '*Middlemarch* and History', *Nineteenth-CenturyFiction*, Vol. 25, 1970, pp. 417–31.

F. W. H. Myers, 'George Eliot', *Century Magazine*, Vol. 23, Nov. 1881, pp. 57–63.

L. Poston, 'Setting and Theme in *Romola*', *Nineteenth-Century Fiction*, Vol. 20, 1966, pp. 355–66.

E. Rubenstein, 'A Forgotten Tale by George Eliot', *Nineteenth-Century Fiction*, Vol. 17, 1963, pp. 175–83. On *The Lifted Veil*.

J. Sudrann, '*Daniel Deronda* and the Landscape fo Exile', *English Literary History*, Vol. 37, 1970, pp. 433–55.

D. Van Ghent, '*Adam Bede*' in *The English Novel: Form and Function*, Holt, New York, 1953, pp. 171–81. Reprinted in Haight.

B. Willey, *Nineteenth-Century Studies: Coleridge to Matthew Arnold*, Section on George Eliot, pp. 204–36, Chatto, London 1960. Reprinted in Haight.

UNPUBLISHED DISSERTATIONS:

Where these are available on film I have included the *Dissertation and Abstracts* order Number.

W. Baker, *The Jewish Elements of George Eliot's Daniel Deronda: A Study of George Eliot's Interest in and Knowledge of Judaism*, M. Phil., London University, 1970.

J. D. Barry, *The Literary Reputation of George Eliot*, Ph.D., Northwestern University, 1955, D.A., 13,066.

J. C. Pratt, *A Middlemarch Miscellany: An Edition, With Introduction and Notes of George Eliot's 1868-1871 Notebook*, Ph.D., Princeton University, 1965, D.A., 65–13,162.

J. R. Quick, *A Critical Edition of George Eliot's Silas Marner*, Ph.D., Yale University, 1968, D.A., 69–8410.

G. A. Santengelo, *The Background of George Eliot's Romola*, Ph.D., University of North Carolina, 1962, D.A., 63–3514.

C. A. Secor, *The Poems of George Eliot: A Critical Edition With Introduction and Notes*, Ph.D., Cornell University, 1970, D.A., 30: 5457–58A.